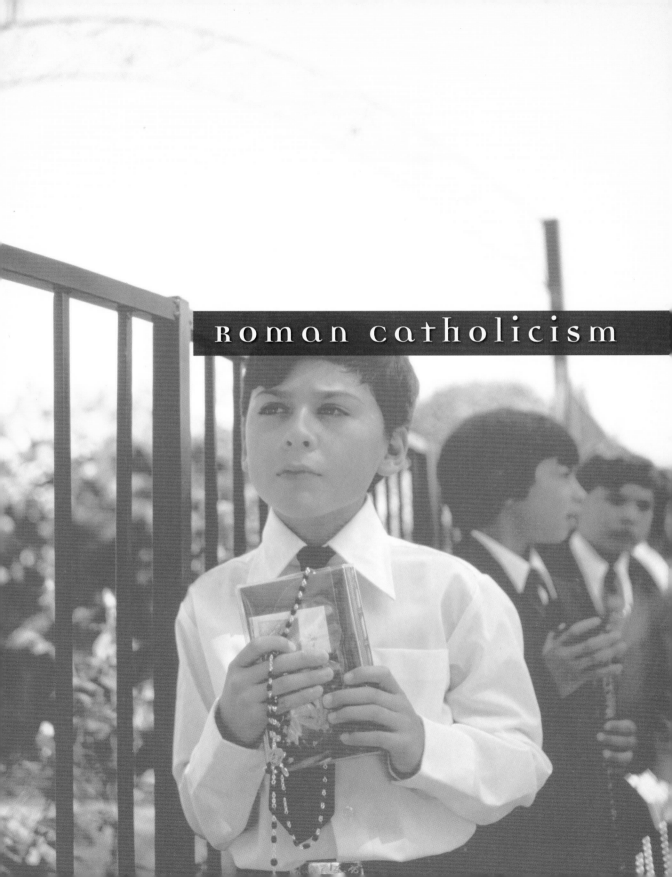

roman catholicism

roman catholicism

STEVEN OTFINOSKI

Marshall Cavendish
Benchmark
New York

To my dear friend Father Basil of the Calmodolese Hermits of Monte Corona, whose keen intellect, warm support, and vast knowledge of the Catholic Church were invaluable in the writing of this book.

Marshall Cavendish Benchmark • 99 White Plains Road • Tarrytown, NY 10591-9001 • www.marshallcavendish.us
Copyright © 2007 by Marshall Cavendish Corporation • All rights reserved. No part of this book may be reproduced or utilized in any form or by any means electronic or mechanical, including photocopying, recording, or by any information storage and retrieval system, without permission from the copyright holders. • All Internet sites were available and accurate when the book was sent to press. • Library of Congress Cataloging-in-Publication Data • Otfinoski, Steven. • Roman Catholicism / by Steven Otfinoski. p. cm. - (World religions) • Summary: "An exploration of the origins and history, basic tenets and beliefs, organizations and structure, practices, influence, and contemporary role of the Catholic Church"—Provided by publisher. Includes bibliographical references and index. • ISBN-13: 978-0-7614-2119-1 ISBN-10: 0-7614-2119-X 1. Catholic Church. I. Title. II. Series: World religions (Marshall Cavendish Benchmark) BX891.3.O84 2006 282-dc22 2005019715

Series design by Sonia Chaghatzbanian • Cover photo: Stephanie Maze/Corbis

The photographs in this book are used by permission and through the courtesy of: *Corbis*: Stephanie Maze, 1, 3, 4-5, 6-7, 97; Owen Franklin, 2; Max Rossi Reuters, 8; National Gallery Collection; By kind permission of the Truteess of the National Gallery, London, 24; Alinari Archives, 46; Summerfield Press, 50; Reuters, 56; Norbert Schaefer, 59; Bob Krist, 66; Sygma, 72; Richard T. Nowitz, 79; Reuters, 81; M. Meyer/zefa, 88; Rob Howard, 94; David Lees, back cover. *Art Resource, New York:* Scala, 18, 20, 30; Alinari, 28.

Printed in China • 1 3 5 6 4 2

contents

roman catholicism

Pope John Paul II, infirm and aged, gazes from the window of his private apartment on a white dove, one of two released by children at the Vatican on January 30, 2005. Moments earlier, he had delivered a message of peace to a crowd below in Saint Peter's Square. Just six weeks later, this much beloved pope would be dead.

INTRODUCTION

Rome had rarely seen such a week in its more than 2,500-year history. Two to three million pilgrims from around the world flooded its narrow streets and plazas, more than doubling the city's population and causing headaches for police and other authorities. They had come to mourn the death and celebrate the life of the man who had presided over the world's largest Church for twenty-six years—Pope John Paul II.

For three days an unending procession of Christians and many non-Christians waited in line for up to twenty-four hours to get a brief glimpse of the deceased pope. Then on Friday, April 8, 2005, the week reached its climax with a funeral in Saint Peter's Square that was unprecedented in size and attendance. Among the millions present were some one hundred world leaders from about eighty countries, including U.S. president George W. Bush and two former American presidents. Millions more around the world watched the funeral on television. But along with the grief and mourning, there was curiosity and excitement about who the next pope would be. Within two weeks the cardinals of the Catholic Church would meet to elect a new leader. For, no matter how much John Paul II would be missed, the Church would go on, as it had for two thousand years, with a new pontiff (or pope) at its head.

The Roman Catholic Church is the largest religious institution in the world today. There are about 1.1 billion Catholics worldwide, including about half of all Christians, followers of Jesus. Catholics live and worship in every part of the world. The greatest numbers of them reside in Europe and Latin America. The United States is home to 67 million Catholics, making it the country with the fourth-largest number of Catholics. The Catholic Church is the richest and, perhaps, the most influential of the world's religious institutions. Its head, the pope, is the world's most powerful religious leader.

Yet, at the dawn of the twenty-first century, the Roman Catholic Church is facing one of the greatest crises in its two-thousand-year history. Charges against priests of sexually abusing children in the United States, Canada, Europe, and elsewhere have made international headlines since early 2002. This betrayal of trust from men meant to be Jesus's representative in the world has tarnished the Church's image for many. Settlements in many of these sex abuse cases have cost the Church millions of dollars, causing an economic strain.

There are other problems facing the Church today. The number of young men entering the priesthood has been steadily shrinking for several decades, causing a severe shortage of priests in North America and elsewhere. The number of Roman Catholic parishes in the United States has declined from 19,331 in 1995 to 19,081 in 2003, due in large part to a population shift from urban areas to the suburbs. At a time of world change and turmoil, the Catholic Church often seems out of step with the modern world. A number of Catholics, particularly in the United States, choose not to agree with the Church's stand against artificial birth control, homosexuality, and embryonic stem-cell research, among other issues. At the same time, more traditional Catholics have balked since 1971 at the replacement of Latin by modern languages in the Mass, the central Catholic rite. They have also opposed new Church social teachings, such as disapproval of the death penalty and opposition to most wars.

Yet the Church has weathered many crises before and, as the

outpouring of affection after the death of Pope John Paul II showed, it remains a rock of faith and shelter for millions of Catholics around the world. To gain a better understanding of this remarkable Church, we need to look at its long and eventful history, going back two thousand years to the ministry of Jesus, who Catholics believe was, and is, the son of God.

one

ORIGINS AND HISTORY

The Greek word *katholikos,* from which *Catholic* is derived, means "universal." The Catholic Church considers itself universal in a number of senses. It is obligated to spread Roman Catholicism throughout the world and, to some extent, it has done so since the first century C.E. It also seeks to spread Jesus's message of love to people of all nations, backgrounds, and conditions.

jesus christ

Jesus is the Greek form of *Joshua,* meaning "the Lord is salvation." Jesus was born in Bethlehem in Palestine about 6 B.C.E., during the Roman occupation of that land. He was, according to Catholic doctrine, born to a virgin mother, Mary. Her husband, Joseph, was a carpenter. For the first thirty years of his life, Jesus lived in obscurity, probably following Joseph's trade. Then at about age thirty he began a public ministry, roaming from place to place in the region of Galilee, preaching to and teaching Jews, performing miracles, healing the sick, and restoring the dead to life. He drew a small group of lowly disciples around him, choosing as apostles (missionaries) mostly fishermen to help him in his work.

The Jews of Palestine, one of the first peoples to believe in only one God, had for a thousand years been anticipating a Messiah, a divine messenger who would establish God's kingdom on earth. Some believed that Jesus was this Messiah, although he hardly seemed the kingly figure many were looking forward to. He came to be called the Christ, from the Greek word *Christos*, meaning "anointed one." The Jewish religious leaders, including the Pharisees and Sadduccees, felt threatened by Jesus's popularity with the people and plotted to kill him. During the Jewish holiday of Passover, Jesus came to Jerusalem with his followers and was arrested and charged with blasphemy (irreverence). The Roman authorities agreed to prosecute Jesus at the instigation of the leading Jewish rabbis. He was condemned, whipped, and then crucified on a hill called Golgotha in Jerusalem. Christians have generally believed he sacrificed his life for the sins of humankind. On the third day following his death, according to the Gospels—holy writings about Jesus's life by four of his apostles—Mary Magdalene and two other women visited his tomb to anoint his body with spices. They found the body gone and an angel in the tomb who said to them, "Why do you look for the living among the dead? He is not here; he has risen!" (Luke 24: 5–6, meaning the book of Luke, chapter 24, verses 5 through 6). The part of the Bible, the Catholic holy book, called the New Testament reports many appearances of the risen Jesus. His resurrection from the dead is a cornerstone of Christian faith.

The first christians

Jesus was born a Jew and remained one until his death. His twelve apostles were also Jews. After his death, they preached to other Jews in Jerusalem and eventually all over Palestine. Among the apostles were Matthew, John, and Simon Peter. Before Jesus's death, he chose Peter to be the leader of the Christian Church, the first pope.

Many Jews, however, refused to accept Jesus as the son of God and rejected Christianity. Some actively sought to suppress this small sect. Among them was Saul of Tarsus, a Pharisee (a member of a Jewish sect), who actively and openly persecuted Christians. According to an

The sermon on the mount

Most of what we know about the historical Jesus is contained in four books of the Bible called the Gospels, from a Greek word meaning "good news." Each Gospel is said to be written by a follower of Jesus. They are Matthew, Mark, Luke, and John. The Sermon on the Mount, included in the Gospel of Matthew (chapters 5, 6, and 7), is the longest recorded sermon given by Jesus. It contains the essential parts of his teachings and forms many core Christian beliefs.

The sermon, probably delivered from a hilltop to a multitude of people, begins with a series of blessings for those who were looked on with favor by Jesus, but who are often misused or ignored by the world. These blessings are called the beatitudes and here are five of them:

> **Blessed are the poor in spirit,**
> **For theirs is the kingdom of heaven.**
> **Blessed are the meek,**
> **For they will inherit the earth.**
> **Blessed are those who hunger and thirst for righteousness,**
> **For they will be filled.**
> **Blessed are the pure in heart,**
> **For they will see God.**
> **Blessed are those who are persecuted because of righteousness**
> **For theirs is the kingdom of heaven.   (Matthew 5:2, 5–6, 8, 10)**

Later in his sermon, Jesus preached a message of love for all people and urged those who follow him to avoid hypocrisy, seek goodness, scorn the outward shows of worldly wealth, and help the poor and needy. Here are some more quotations:

> **You have heard that it was said, 'Love your neighbor and hate your enemy.' But I tell you: Love your enemies and pray for those who persecute you, that you may be sons of your Father in heaven. (Matthew 5: 43-45)**

> **Why do you look at the speck of sawdust in your brother's eye and pay no attention to the plank in your own eye? How can you say to your brother, 'Let me take the speck out of your eye,' when all the time there is a plank in your own eye? (Matthew 7: 3–4)**

> **Ask and it will be given to you, seek and you will find, knock and the door will be opened to you. For everyone who asks receives, he who seeks finds, and to him who knocks, the door will be opened. (Matthew 7: 7–8)**

account repeated three times in the book of the New Testament called the Acts of the Apostles, Saul experienced a dramatic conversion to Christianity while traveling to Damascus, Syria, to arrest more Christians. Soon afterward, he became a leading Christian proselytizer and changed his name to Paul.

Although Peter and the other original apostles supposed the gospel should be preached only to Jews, Paul wanted to convert gentiles, non-Jews. He traveled outside Palestine into Asia Minor (Turkey), the Mediterranean world of Greece, and eventually to Rome itself. Everywhere he and his companions went they established Christian communities. It was soon clear that if the Christian Church was to grow, it would be in the larger world of the gentiles.

Paul wrote letters called epistles to the various church communities that he founded to encourage them and to correct what he saw as their errors of faith and doctrine. These Epistles were later collected and, along with the four Gospels, make up a large portion of the Bible's New Testament.

Paul, Peter, and other apostles paid a heavy price for their discipleship. The Romans considered them traitors because they refused to obey the Roman state, its gods, and its emperor. They were arrested, tried, condemned, and executed.

The church in Rome

Many early Christians became martyrs as did the first disciples during the first and second centuries of the Common Era. Persecution of Christians ebbed and peaked according to the whims of the current Roman emperor and the fickle public. It reached its bloodiest heights during the reigns of Nero (54–68) and Diocletian (284–305). Under these tyrants' orders, captured Christians were imprisoned, burned to death, or thrown into outdoor amphitheaters like the Roman Coliseum to be devoured by hungry lions for the amusement of Roman spectators.

saint paul's three journeys of faith

Paul's legendary three missionary journeys planted the first Christian churches outside Palestine. Paul had established a base in Antioch in Syria. Later he sailed to the island of Cyprus with his friend Barnabas. When Paul's speech in a synagogue in Antioch of Pisidia was angrily rejected by Jews there, he made the historic decision to bring his message to gentiles.

His second journey took Paul for the first time to the mainland of Europe at Macedonia. At the town of Philippi he was thrown into prison for "disturbing the peace" with his preaching and was freed by an earthquake that broke open the prison. After hostile Jews drove him out of Thessalonica, another Macedonian city, Paul sailed to Greece. He made few converts in Athens, but established a thriving church at Corinth, where he stayed eighteen months.

Paul's third and final journey covered much of the same territory as his second journey. He worked to revitalize and reform Christian communities he had already established. When he was again attacked by Jews in Jerusalem, he was taken into protective custody by Roman soldiers. He demanded, as a Roman citizen, to be sent to Rome to be tried. Paul eventually arrived in Rome, where he remained a prisoner. He was beheaded by the civil authorities in Rome in the year 64 or 67 C.E.

Despite widespread persecution, Christianity continued to grow and spread. With the deaths of the original leaders of the faith, their specially chosen successors, called bishops, were installed in each major Christian community and were responsible for the welfare of that community's members.

In 313 Roman emperor Constantine I, also known as Constantine the Great (reign 306–337), issued the Edict of Milan, which granted Christians the right to practice their faith. Constantine's motives in doing so may have been as much political as humanitarian. The Roman empire was in decline, fraught with corruption and immorality. By legalizing Christianity, Constantine may have hoped to revive Roman society with the new religion's energy and spirit.

Rome soon became the center of the Christian Church, and by 350 there were nearly 34 million Christians, making up more than half of the population of the Roman empire. Just as the spiritual values articulated by Greek philosophers such as Plato influenced the new religion, so did Roman law and organization. The bishop of Rome presided over the Church, ranking higher than the patriarchs (important bishops or religious leaders) of such other major Christian communities as Antioch in Syria and Alexandria in Egypt. In 330 Constantine moved the capital from Rome to a new city in Asia Minor (now Turkey) which he named Constantinople. A new and eventually mostly eastern patriarchate, or spiritual community, was established there that would, in time, grow apart from the Roman Church.

One of Constantine's successors, Theodosius I (379–395) established Christianity as the Roman's state religion in 392 and banned pagan worship. After the death of Theodosius, the empire permanently split into the western Roman empire, centered in Rome, and the eastern Roman empire, centered in Constantinople.

A Literary Flowering

In the fourth and fifth centuries, Christianity experienced a renaissance (rebirth). A number of Christian thinkers and writers called Fathers of the Church helped to establish the foundations of what would become the Roman Catholic Church. Two of the most important of these writers were Saint Augustine (354–430) and Saint Jerome (about 340–420?).

Augustine was born in Roman North Africa to a Christian mother and a pagan father. He grew up to become a teacher and led a pagan, somewhat dissolute life until he converted to Christianity in his early thirties. He became a priest and in 396 was appointed the bishop of Hippo in North Africa.

Of Augustine's many writings, the most influential were his

Augustine's influential writings gave momentum, definition, and cohesion to the slowly mobilizing Church.

Confessions (about 400), a spiritual autobiography of great power, and *The City of God* (413–426), a book that made a convincing argument for a single united church and the working of divine providence in history.

Jerome was born in what today is called Yugoslavia. He traveled to the Near East as a young man. Living in the desert for several years as a monk led him to devote all his attention to his Christian writing. He is best known for his commentaries on biblical texts and his accurate translation of the Bible into Latin, known as the Vulgate, which largely replaced a previous translation. It remained for many years the standard Bible of Catholicism.

A third figure who helped to consolidate and strengthen the still-growing Christian Church was Pope Leo I (about 440–461). He affirmed the power of the papacy, preached eloquently on Christian faith, successfully combated heresies (a belief or practice contrary to Christian doctrine) that threatened Church unity, and convinced Attila the Hun (406?–453) and Genseric (died 477), king of the Vandals, not to invade and destroy Rome.

His greatest work, called *Tome to Flavian*, explained the orthodox or accepted view that Jesus was one divine person, possessing both divine and human natures. When the bishops assembled for the Council of Chalcedon in 451 heard the *Tome* read, they cried out: "Peter [the first pope] has spoken through Leo!"

But, in the end, the Church and its leaders could not save Rome from invasion. In 476 the German general Odoacer (about 476–493) deposed the last emperor of Rome. Europe entered a period of chaos and division, from which the Roman Catholic Church would emerge more powerful than before.

The conversion of western Europe

The barbarian tribes that overran most of western Europe in the sixth and seventh centuries were either Arian heretics who denied

Saint Jerome, one of the great literary figures of the early Church, is seen at his scholarly pursuits in this famous painting by the Italian artist Michelangelo Caravaggio. Note the skull, a grim reminder to Jerome of his mortality.

the divinity of Jesus or were non-Christian pagans. One of the first strongholds of Christianity in Europe outside Italy was Ireland, parts of which were converted by Saint Patrick in the fifth century. During the sixth century, Christianity was adopted by one kingdom after another—the Franks in Gaul (later France), the Visigoths in Spain, and the Anglo-Saxons in England.

The greatest ruler of the era, the Frankish king Charlemagne (768–814), became a champion of Christianity and extended its influence as he conquered much of Europe. On Christmas Day, 800, Pope Leo III (reign 795–816) crowned Charlemagne the emperor of the Romans. Church and state had become collaborators. Charlemagne's kingdom in 962 was declared the Holy Roman empire and would remain on the map of Europe for more than eight hundred years.

The papacy and monasticism

While kings ruled the emerging nation-states in the Middle Ages (500–1500), all nations were spiritually subject to the Church and papal authority.

The Christian monk, a man who renounced the world and lived with others in a largely self-sufficient religious community called a monastery, became the model for all Christians. The father of Western monasticism was Saint Benedict (480–547), who founded the Benedictine Order in 529. His Rule of Saint Benedict established the monastic life of prayer, work, meals, and study that is still followed by many monastic orders.

By the twelfth century, there were no less than two thousand monasteries in western Europe operated by more than a dozen different religious orders. The monastery was a "church within the church," and many of them were known for their great wealth, spiritual riches, and scholarship. Learning was preserved in the monastery by the monastic copyist. He made elaborate, often incredibly artful, copies of the Bible and other essential religious texts. It could take one monk more than a year to copy the Bible, and the work was painstaking. But the monk copyists did their work without complaint because, as one of them put it, "for every letter, line, and point, a sin is forgiven me."

The great schism and the crusades

The early Church was made up of two principal parts, in the eastern Roman empire and the western. From the outset, these two Churches had different viewpoints. Heresies, schisms (differences), the interference of emperors, and invasions of Muslims—religious followers of the Arab prophet Muhammad (about 570–632)— weakened the Eastern or Byzantine Church. There had been many quarrels between East and West that had been patched up, such as the split in 863 between Pope Nicholas I (858–867) and Photius (858– 867, 878–886), the patriarch (head of the church) of Constantinople in 863. Relations between the two Churches grew progressively worse, and in 1054 they split permanently. Delegates of Pope Leo IX (1049–1054) excommunicated Michael I Celularius, patriarch of Constantinople, for defiling bread used in Holy Communion in the city's Latin chapels. Celularius in turn excommunicated them. After a thousand years of general unity, the Christian Church was no longer unified. The Western Church came to be called the Roman Catholic Church, and the Eastern Church became known as the Orthodox Church.

But relations between the two Churches were not completely cut off. About 1090, Byzantine emperor Alexius I Comnenus (reign 1081–1118) asked Pope Urban II (about 1088–1099) to help defeat the Turks, who were persecuting Christian pilgrims to Palestine— which is considered by Christians to be the Holy Land where Jesus had lived and died. At the Council of Clermont in France in 1095 the pope called for Christian warriors to march to the Holy Land and take back the city of Jerusalem from the Muslim Turks. Thousands of

The sistine chapel—michelangelo's masterpiece

For centuries, the Church had inspired, encouraged, and supported great art, music, and literature. One of the greatest works of religious art is the frescoes created by the Italian artist Michelangelo (1475–1564) for the Vatican's Sistine Chapel. The chapel, built in 1473, remains the most famous palace in Vatican City (the independent state where the pope lives) and is the place where the cardinals come to elect a new pope.

Pope Julius II (1503–1513) commissioned Michelangelo in 1508 to paint the chapel's walls and ceiling. Over the next four and a half years, the artist labored, producing three magnificent scenes from the Old Testament—the Creation of the World, the fall of Adam and Eve, and Noah and the Flood. He went on to paint *The Last Judgment* on the wall above the chapel's altar. This enormous work is 60 feet (18.3 meters) high and 30 feet (9.2 meters) wide.

Centuries of dust and smoke from the chapel's candles obscured the greatness of Michelangelo's work. A major cleanup of the walls and ceiling was begun in 1980, and lasted fourteen years. It restored the frescoes of the Sistine Chapel to their original clarity and breathtaking beauty.

European soldiers and knights rallied to the cry *Deus vult*, Latin for "God wills it."

Urban II's motives were only partly religious. He hoped to bring greater glory and power to the Church and also give warring European nations a common foe to unite against. In this way, the first Crusade (1095–1099) began. The word *crusade* is derived from the Latin *crux*, for "cross," because of the crosses the crusaders sewed onto their clothing. The first Crusade was a partial success. The knights took back Jerusalem from the Turks, but less than fifty years later the Turks reclaimed part of the lands they had lost. A second Crusade

Saint Thomas Aquinas upholds the Church and Scripture in this symbolic fifteenth-century image from an Italian altarpiece. The Catholic Church regards Aquinas as its greatest theologian who definitively summarized Catholic beliefs in his masterwork *Summa Theologiae*.

was organized but failed to drive back the Turks. When they seized Jerusalem in 1187 under their great leader Saladin (about 1174–1193), a third Crusade was begun. King Richard the Lionhearted of England (1189–1199) was one of its leaders. Although he led the crusaders to victory in numerous battles, he was unable to recapture Jerusalem. Richard did manage to convince the Muslims to allow Christian pilgrims to enter the city in peace.

There would be five more Crusades over the next century, but none had the impact of the first three. In the end, the Crusades accomplished little militarily, but they did strengthen the power of the Church and the pope in the West and encouraged Europeans to travel to and explore other lands for trade and colonization.

The Rise of Scholasticism

In the thirteenth century, the Church experienced its greatest intellectual rebirth since the days of Saint Augustine. Leading men of learning, called scholastics or school men, used the classical system of reasoning developed by the ancient Greeks to prove the existence of God and reaffirm Church doctrine. The major scholastic writers and thinkers were Albertus Magnus (about 1200–1280) of Germany and his follower Thomas Aquinas (1225–1274) of Italy. Aquinas's great work, *Summa Theologiae* (1266–1273), was a brilliant summation of Christian theology that is still the acknowledged foundation for Catholic teaching. Some of its best-known passages give five proofs of the existence of God. Another scholastic, the Englishman Roger Bacon (about1220–1292), encouraged Christians to pursue the worthy studies of science and mathematics.

The ferment of inquiry in the Church also led to the founding of the first universities of Europe. The University of Bologna in Italy was the first, established about 1100. About a century later, the University of Paris, the center of scholasticism, opened its doors.

Another cultural landmark of medieval Europe was the great churches or cathedrals built in the ornate style known as Gothic. These grand houses of worship were awe inspiring. They had high rib-vaulted ceilings, brilliantly colored stained glass windows illustrating biblical stories, and ornate sculptures that studded their exteriors. Gothic cathedrals were more than houses of worship, however. Public meetings were held there and classes taught. Their great entranceways served as gathering places for the common people, where they could mingle and discuss the news of the day. Many of these great cathedrals still stand and continue to inspire worshippers and visitors. The most splendid examples include Notre-Dame in Paris, Westminster Abbey in London, and the Cologne Cathedral in Germany. Officially, a cathedral need be neither large nor grand. It is, by definition, the church of a bishop.

"The Babylonian captivity" and the great schism

The independence of the Church was challenged by the growth of nation-states in western Europe. The powerful princes who ruled the Italian city-states went to war and threatened the existence of the papacy in Rome. In 1305 a French archbishop was elected at Lyons in

Ignatius Loyola and the Jesuits

Since its founding in 1534, the Jesuit Order has remained a powerful force within the Catholic Church. Its founder, Ignatius Loyola (1491–1556), was the privileged son of a noble Spanish family. He became a soldier and led a life of ambition, anger, and pride until a cannon blast shattered one leg and ended his military career. While recovering from his injuries, Loyola read the Bible and the lives of the saints and was inspired to become a soldier for Jesus. He founded the Society of Jesus with only six disciples. Intellectually rigorous and loyally devoted to the pope, the Jesuits quickly grew in numbers. By the time of Loyola's death, there were more than one thousand Jesuits.

Despite their great accomplishments in education and missionary work, the Jesuits were viewed with jealousy and suspicion by many inside and outside the Church who felt threatened by their secrecy and growing influence. They were suppressed or expelled in one country after another, until Pope Clement XIV (1769–1774) banned them entirely in 1773. The order was revived forty-one years later.

Today the Jesuits are one of the more influential orders in the Catholic Church, having the largest number of male clergy. They operate more than four thousand schools, colleges, and universities internationally and have left their mark in science, theology, literature, and exploration.

France and took the name Pope Clement V. Four years later, Clement moved the papal center from Rome to Avignon in southern France. Four successive popes would reside in Avignon for the next sixty-eight years. Those Christians who were disturbed by the influence of the French kings over the papacy called the period the "Babylonian captivity," referring to the seventy-year exile of Jerusalem's Jews in Babylon from 586 to 516 B.C.E. In 1377 Pope Gregory XI (1370–1378) returned the papacy to Rome.

Following Gregory's death in 1378, Church leaders elected Pope

Urban VI (1378–1389). The election was later declared invalid, and a French cardinal was named Pope Clement VII (1378–1394). Germany, Italy, and much of northern Europe supported Urban as pope, while Spain and France believed Clement to be the true pope. A third claimant to the papacy, Alexander V, followed in 1409. In what came to be called the Great Western Schism, Urban, Clement, and Alexander all claimed to be the legitimate pope and simultaneously ruled in Rome, Avignon, and the Italian city of Pisa. This unseemly spectacle would last until 1415, when the Council of Constance deposed Alexander's successor, John XXIII (1410–1415), and elected Martin V (1417–1431) as pope two years later. The new Roman pope was accepted by all sides, and the Church was once again united.

As the Middle Ages were drawing to a close, a rebirth of learning and discovery called the Renaissance was sweeping across Europe. New ideas about politics, warfare, and statecraft were turning the Church into an earthly kingdom. Popes became more interested in worldly wealth and power than in maintaining their spiritual leadership. Some bishops and priests became lazy and corrupt. The model for these Church leaders was the worldly Renaissance prince rather than Jesus Christ. The Church was overdue for reform.

The Reformation

Martin Luther (1483–1546) was a German monk who was greatly troubled by the corruption and worldliness of the Church. On October 31, 1517, Luther nailed Ninety-five Theses (propositions) criticizing the Church's practices onto the door of the castle church in Wittenberg, Germany. At the time, Luther had no intention of breaking away from the Church, but hoped to reform it from within. When the Church resisted his reforms, Luther advocated a split. Luther especially targeted the selling of indulgences by churchmen. That was how sinners could pay to have their punishments in the afterlife reduced. Luther also

Martin Luther's questioning of corruption within the Church eventually led to the Protestant Reformation. However, Luther, a devout Catholic monk, originally did not intend to break away from the Church but only to help correct its mistakes.

questioned the supremacy of the pope and the worship of the Virgin Mary and the saints, which he compared to idolatry. He sought to bring Christianity back to the simplicity and traditions of the early Christian Church in which the Bible—the word of God—was the final authority for Christians everywhere.

The Church sought to avoid a direct conflict with Luther and his growing number of followers but decided it had to face him or jeopardize its future. In a bull (decree) in 1520, Pope Leo X (1513–1521) censured forty-one of Luther's ninety-five propositions and told him that he had sixty days to withdraw these or face excommunication (expulsion from the Church). When put on trial, Luther bravely declared: "Unless I am convicted by Scripture or by right reason . . . I neither can nor will recant anything, since it is neither right nor safe to act against conscience, God help me. Amen."

The split was final. Some called this the Reformation Protestantism, inspired by Luther and other religious thinkers, which swept across northern Europe, becoming the principal religion in parts of Germany, the Scandinavian countries, Great Britain, and large sections of central Europe. Catholicism remained the main religion in Italy, Spain, and France.

The counter-Reformation

The Catholic Church tried to combat Protestantism by reforming and strengthening itself. The so-called Counter-Reformation began with the Council of Trent (1545–1563), one of the most significant Church councils. Clergy banned many abuses of the Church, including the misuse of funds. Monks were forced to give up their concubines, and bishops were commanded to end their lavish lifestyles. Ecclesiastical laws and monastic rules were defined more strictly, seminary training was required for priestly ordination, Catholic education was encouraged, and missionary

During the Saint Bartholomew's Day Massacre on August 24, 1572, French Catholics killed hundreds of Protestants in Paris. The order for the slaughter was given by King Charles IX, who was Catholic and feared that the Protestants, called Huguenots, were about to seize the government.

work in foreign lands was undertaken. Much of this work was given to the new order of the Society of Jesus, whose members, the Jesuits, became the driving force behind the Counter-Reformation.

The desire for reform led to widespread persecution of heretics and Protestants. The Inquisition, first established by Pope Gregory IX (1227–1241) in Germany in 1231, and later in France and Italy, was a powerful civil tribunal of Church authorities who interrogated and put on trial those accused of heresy. Physical torture was used as a frequent tool, as it was in all judicial proceedings of the time, to obtain confessions. Some of those convicted of heresy were burned at the stake. The deadly determination of the Church's inquisitors was summed up grimly by Pope Paul IV (1555–1559), who claimed, "Even if my own father were a heretic, I would gather wood to burn him."

The Second Vatican Council's (Vatican II's) 1965 Decree on Religious Liberty laid down guiding principles to evaluate those past episodes and make sure that they do not occur again. In 2004 the Catholic Church released a study entitled *The Inquisition,* which was based on years of research by fifty historians. It claimed that the number of victims of the Inquisition was fewer than had once been thought. For example, between 1540 and 1700, historical records indicate that about 2,250 people were executed in Spain rather than the tens or hundreds of thousands once thought.

The church goes to war

The Inquisition was not the only tool of terror used against Protestants. On August 24, 1572, Saint Bartholomew's Day, French Protestants—called Huguenots—were slaughtered by Catholics in the streets of Paris. The Saint Bartholomew's Day Massacre was followed by widespread attacks on Huguenots throughout France. In six weeks about ten thousand Protestants were killed.

The persecution was not one-sided. In England, Henry VIII (1509–1547) established the Church of England, which was Protestant. He mercilessly persecuted English Catholics, as did his daughter, Elizabeth I (1558–1603), and her successors for more than a century.

The fight between Catholics and Protestants culminated in the Thirty Years War (1618–1648) that pitted Protestant German states, Denmark, and Sweden against the Catholic Hapsburg rulers of Spain, Austria, Italy, and the German Catholic states. The war ended in the Peace of Westphalia that granted independence to the Protestant states, much to the outrage of the pope, who was against the treaty. But the world was becoming a far more secular (nonreligious) place, and the pope's fiery statements in opposition to the treaty were ignored by the nations' leaders.

The church in Retreat

The Catholic Church had made its peace, in a way, with Protestantism, but now faced a new challenge on its own ground. The kings of France, Austria, Spain, and other Catholic countries felt that they, and not the pope in Rome, should control the Catholic churches in their own countries. At the same time, religion—and the Catholic Church in particular—was coming under increasing attack from thinkers and writers in what came to be called the Age of Reason. That period in Europe, stretching from the seventeenth century to the late eighteenth century, was marked by a belief that human reason alone could right the wrongs of the world and create a better society. For the French writer Voltaire (1694–1778), a leader of the movement, religion was little more than superstition that kept the mass of people in their place, while the clergy grew fat and wealthy.

This anti-religious feeling reached a fever pitch during the French Revolution (1787–1799), when the Church was seen as an enemy of the people, aligned with the aristocracy and the monarchy. Priests were imprisoned, exiled, removed from office, and sometimes executed by the revolutionaries. Monasteries and churches were seized by the state and their wealth confiscated. For a brief time, atheism became the "state religion" of France. After Napoléon Bonaparte (1769–1821) came to power in France, he reinstated the Church, but the empire he came to rule over was wholly secular. The Church, once an independent entity, was now under the authority of the state. To exert his power further, in 1809 Napoléon seized the Papal States—territory in central Italy that had belonged to the Church for centuries—and took Pope Pius VII (1800–1830) captive.

The nineteenth century saw the Church rejected by an increasingly nonreligious world. The restoration of the Jesuits in 1814 and the return of the Papal States the following year brought some renewal of vigor and energy to Catholicism. The establishment of the Catholic Union in 1843 in Germany sought to help the Church find ways to play a meaningful role in the modern world. But the papacy in the late nineteenth century looked with suspicion at the growing secularism that conducted civil policy outside a religious context. Pope Pius IX (1846–1878), who began his long reign as a reformer, ended up an extreme reactionary after revolution in Italy forced him to flee for his life. Pius IX also presided over the first Vatican Council (Vatican I, 1869–1870), which defined the doctrine of papal infallibility (that the pope was incapable of making a mistake in matters of belief).

In 1878 Leo XIII (1878–1903) became pope and worked to reverse the decline of the Church and its influence in the modern world. He reached out to befriend the liberal governments and the working classes with some success. In his encyclical (a letter to all his bishops), *Rerum Novarum*, he gave his approval to labor unions, finding common ground with the average working person. The Roman Catholic Church entered the new century with both misgiving and a sense of hope for the future.

The catholic church in the Americas

On his second voyage to the New World in 1494, Christopher Columbus (1451–1506) had a dozen missionaries on board. For the Spanish, Portuguese, and French explorers of the Americas, converting the native peoples to Christianity was believed to be as important as finding precious metals and establishing colonies. By 1530 there were three episcopal sees, or religious centers, in Spanish America—in the present-day Dominican Republic, Cuba, and Mexico. The first Roman Catholic Mass in the present-day United States was celebrated by the Spanish at Saint Augustine, Florida, on September 8, 1565.

Spanish missionaries in the American Southwest and Southeast also established missions: communities where Indians were educated, converted to Christianity, and taught skills that helped support the mission. Father Junipero Serra (1713–1784) began establishing a string of missions along the coast of California in the mid-eighteenth century.

Catholicism was slower to take root in the thirteen English colonies, especially in New England, where the Puritans, strict English Protestants, established the Congregational Church. The aristocratic Calvert family of England founded the colony of Maryland in 1634 as a haven for European Catholics. In 1649 Maryland passed one of the first laws granting religious freedom in America for all Christians. This Maryland law later inspired the religious freedom decreed by the U.S. Constitution.

In 1789 John Carroll (1735–1815), a Maryland-born Jesuit priest, was appointed the first Roman Catholic bishop in the United States at Baltimore, Maryland. At that time there were 30,000 Catholics in the

ɛlizɑbɛth ɑnn sɛton

Elizabeth Ann Bayley was born in New York City in 1774 to a wealthy colonial family. She married William Seton, a rich merchant, in 1794. The Setons had five children and were living a happy and prosperous life in America when tragedy struck. Seton's business went bankrupt, and he became seriously ill with tuberculosis. With his wife, he traveled to Italy in 1803 in search of a cure. He died there that same year, and Elizabeth felt drawn to the Catholic Church, which comforted and supported her. On her return to America, she converted to Catholicism. In 1809 at the request of a French priest, she opened the first Catholic elementary school for girls in Baltimore.

On fire with her newfound faith, Seton became a nun and founded an order of nuns—the Sisters of Charity of Saint Joseph, in Emmitsburg, Maryland, which became the order's headquarters. She taught her novices: ". . . the first end I propose in our daily work is to do the will of God; secondly, to do it in the *manner* He wills; and thirdly, to do it *because* it is His will." Seton's efforts established community service as an important part of Catholic life in the United States. She died in 1821 of the same disease, tuberculosis, that had killed her husband. Her nephew James Roosevelt Bayley later became the first bishop of Newark, New Jersey, and founded Seton Hall College in 1856 in her honor. Now called Seton Hall University, it was the first Catholic college in the United States operated by a diocese—the Church itself—and not a religious order. In 1975 Elizabeth Seton was canonized and became the first American-born saint of the Catholic Church.

United States, more than half of them living in Maryland. The same year Bishop Carroll founded a Catholic-run university in Washington, D.C., that would later become Georgetown University.

From 1789 to 1850, more than two million Catholic immigrants came to the United States from Europe. The greatest number were from Ireland and Germany. The Irish established themselves as the dominant group in the Catholic Church in the United States, forming the highest percentage of priests in many cities.

In the late 1800s and early 1900s, a second wave of immigrants, this time from southern and eastern Europe, brought three million Catholics to the United States. Many of these immigrants were poor and were seen as a threat by the more established and wealthy Protestant Americans. By the 1920s, racist groups largely composed of white Protestants, such as the Ku Klux Klan, persecuted the Catholics as well as the African Americans and Jews in their communities.

In 1928 Democrat Al Smith (1873–1944), governor of New York, became the first Catholic candidate from a major political party to run for president. Smith was accused by Protestants of being under the control of the pope in Rome. He vehemently denied the charges, responding in a magazine article that, although he was a devout Catholic, "I recognize no power in the institution of my Church to interfere with the operations of the Constitution of the United States or the enforcement of the law of the land. . . ." Nevertheless, Smith lost the election to Republican Herbert Hoover (1874–1964). Thirty-two years later Catholics were more fully accepted in American society, and Catholic John F. Kennedy (1917–1963) of Massachusetts was elected president. Catholic Americans had become a powerful and influential segment of the population politically, socially, and economically.

The Church Enters the Twentieth Century

The reign of Pope Pius X (1903–1914) illustrated the ambivalence of the Church toward the cataclysmic changes of the twentieth century. Pius X was in many ways committed to change and meaningful reform in the areas of caring for the poor, Church music, and ecclesiastical laws. Yet at the same time, he was adamantly opposed to the Modernist movement growing within the Church that asserted that the religious experience was subjective and highly personal and not determined by reason and doctrine. A strong advocate of peace in Europe, Pius X died shortly after the outbreak of World War I.

After the reign of Benedict XV (1914–1922), who died penniless because of his lavish charity to the poor, Pius XI (1922–1939) opposed the rise of Fascism in Italy and Nazism in Germany. However, in 1929 he negotiated with Italian dictator Benito Mussolini (1883–1945) to establish the Church's rule over Vatican City, papal headquarters and the last remnant of the once vast Papal States. Pius XI may well have waited too long to condemn anti-Semitism (hatred of Jews) in Italy and Germany under the Nazi dictatorship of Adolph Hitler (1889–1945).

When World War II broke out in 1939, the Church, then under the rule of Pope Pius XII (1939–1958), maintained its neutrality. About 800,000 Jews were saved from death through his efforts. However, some historians think that the pope could have saved the lives of many more Jews by taking a more active role in the war. His apologists (supporters) state that any harder line against Hitler would have been counterproductive and perhaps have resulted in a greater persecution of Italian Jews.

catholicism versus communism

When the war ended with German and Japanese defeat, the Soviet Union moved into Eastern Europe and took over many of the countries previously controlled by the Nazis. Soviet Communists were atheistic and banned Catholic Mass and Catholic education. Those Catholics who continued to practice their faith were often harassed. Priests were arrested and jailed or executed. Churches were converted into warehouses or museums. Yet, Catholics in Eastern Europe managed to meet and worship secretly. The Church survived the attacks of the Communists, thanks to a small group of courageous clergymen, including Stefan Cardinal Wyszynski (1901–1981) of Poland, who found ways to work with their Communist governments without compromising their faith. The Church in Rome took a hard stand against Communism, and Pius XII gained a reputation as an activist anti-Communist pope who championed religious freedom around the world.

good pope john

On the death of Pius XII in 1958, Angelo Roncalli, a seventy-seven-year-old cardinal from Venice, was elected pope and took the name John XXIII (1959–1963). Because of his advanced age, few people expected him to be a very active Church leader. But Pope John surprised them.

Soon after becoming pope, John called for an ecumenical or general council, the first of its kind to be held in nearly a century. Vatican II, as it came to be called, addressed the Church's role in the modern world and brought sweeping changes in Catholic worship.

Although he lived through only the first of four sessions of the council, which lasted from 1962 to 1965, John left his stamp on this historical event. A short, stocky man, John XXIII had a disarmingly candid manner and a sharp sense of humor that people around the world found irresistible. Affectionately referred to as "good Pope John," and later beatified—declared "Blessed"—in his short reign, he became one of the most popular and best-known popes of modern times.

pope paul VI

The man who replaced John XXIII as pope shared his vision of a renewed and revitalized Church. Pope Paul VI (1963–1978) continued to support the work of Vatican II to its conclusion. To spread the message of ecumenicalism—worldwide Christian unity—and peace, Paul traveled tirelessly, more than any previous pope had. In 1964 he became the first pope, surprisingly, to visit the Holy Land. The following year he became the first pope to visit the United States, addressing the United Nations General Assembly in New York City on the issue of world peace.

But not all of Paul's pronouncements were met with widespread enthusiasm. In 1968 he issued an encyclical entitled *Humanae Vitae.* In it, he reaffirmed a traditional teaching now rejected by many Catholics: the immorality of contraception, artificial birth control. Many Catholics, especially in the United States, found the pope's letter unrealistic and irresponsible in the face of a world population explosion and limited resources. Paul's stand against any form of birth control but natural methods, such as checking a woman's temperature as a means of testing her fertility, made him the most criticized pope in a century.

The pope from poland

After the brief thirty-three-day reign of Pope John Paul I (1978), who died in his sleep, the cardinals elected Cardinal Karol Wojtyla

vatican council II

During the three years of Vatican Council II, the eyes of the world were on the Roman Catholic Church, and the results were earthshaking. The council's opening meeting was attended by 2,500 bishops from around the globe. The council proved to be the kind of *aggiornamento,* updating, that Pope John hoped it would be. It allowed the people of individual nations to say the Mass and other rituals in their own languages, instead of Latin, the Church's universal language. It gave a greater role to the laity in the Church. It encouraged respect for and dialogue with non-Catholic Christians and even non-Christians. It concluded with a powerful restatement and clarification of the doctrine of religious liberty.

While many Catholics, especially in North America and Europe, embraced the changes of Vatican II, a few conservative Catholics opposed them. In 1970, retired French archbishop Marcel Lefebvre (1905–1991) founded a group of ultraconservative Catholics called the Priestly Fraternity of Saint Pius X. It condemned Vatican II as heresy. Lefebvre was automatically excommunicated in 1988 when he ordained four men as bishops on his own authority.

as pope. It was a groundbreaking choice. Wojtyla, who took the name John Paul II (1978–2005), was the first pope from Poland, Eastern Europe, or a Communist country. An energetic man of deep beliefs and immense charm and appeal, John Paul II became the most traveled pope of all time, making five visits to his native Poland and many other Communist countries that had never been visited by a pope before.

In 1991 the Soviet Union dissolved, and eastern Europe and the Soviet republics were to pursue democracy and a free market economy. The Catholic and Orthodox churches in eastern Europe experienced a surge of renewed interest and popularity as these countries shed the atheism of their Soviet masters. A new day was dawning for the worldwide Catholic Church, but it would be full of new challenges.

pope john paul II

The first non-Italian pope in more than four centuries and the first pope ever from Eastern Europe, John Paul II was born on May 18, 1920. As a youth, he was a top student and outstanding athlete. His first ambition was not to be a priest but an actor. He played roles in amateur productions and wrote a number of plays. During the chaos of World War II that nearly destroyed his country, Karol Wojtyla, as the future pope was known in those days, decided to enter the priesthood. He was ordained in 1946, a year after the war ended. At that time the Communists were taking over Poland in the wake of the defeated Germans. Wojtyla became a popular teacher at the Catholic University of Lublin and later at the University of Krakow. In 1964 he was made the archbishop of Krakow. He remained a strong anti-Communist through the 1970s and was elected pope in 1978 at age fifty-eight, the youngest pope in more than one hundred years.

Full of energy and fluent in five languages, including Latin, John Paul II was well received on his many trips to dozens of countries. His several trips to Communist Poland energized the Polish people and played a central role in the rise of Solidarity, the workers' organization that eventually brought down that country's Communist regime. John Paul's staunch anti-Communist stand had its price. In 1981 he was seriously wounded by a Turkish terrorist allegedly paid by Communist agents. He thanked the Virgin Mary for slightly deflecting the bullet and saving his life. The shooting occurred on the very day and hour of Mary's supposed appearance in Fatima, Portugal, in 1917. The pope spent three months in a hospital, but eventually made a full recovery.

A conservative and traditionalist on many religious and social issues, John Paul was also a fearless opponent of the death penalty and most wars, including the Iraq War instigated in 2003 by the United States. He did, however, support the United States' efforts to help Iraq achieve political stability. After several years of failing health due to Parkinson's disease and other ailments, Pope John Paul II died on the evening of April 2, 2005, ending one of the longest and most eventful papal reigns in the Church's history.

TWO

BASIC TENETS AND BELIEFS

Like all of the world's great religions, Roman Catholicism, the largest branch of Christianity, has its own set of tenets (or laws) and beliefs. Where do these tenets and beliefs come from? For Catholics, there are two sources: the Bible and Church tradition. These sources are taught and interpreted by the pope and the college (or body) of high churchmen known as bishops. We will examine each of these sources in detail before looking at some of the tenets and beliefs that are derived from them.

The Bible

The Bible is the holy book for both the Jewish and Christian religions. The word *Bible* is derived from the Greek word for "books," and the Catholic Bible is actually seventy-three separate books in one. They are written in a number of different literary forms, including poems, historical narratives, stories, parables, letters, and proverbs. The Bible is divided into two distinct parts—the Old Testament and the New Testament.

The forty-six books of the Old Testament describe events from God's creation of the world to the first century B.C.E. Christians believe God's promises to his chosen people, the Israelites, were fulfilled in Jesus's coming to live on earth. The twenty-seven books of the New Testament describe events from the birth of Jesus to about 100 C.E. They tell about the life and death of Jesus and the development of the early Christian Church under the direction of the first apostles. The Catholic New Testament is divided into four sections: 1. the four Gospels of Jesus's life; 2. the Acts of the Apostles (one book); 3. the Epistles or letters of the apostles (twenty-one books); and 4. the Book of Revelation, which describes events leading up to the Last Judgment on earth, when Jesus returns. Among the forty-six Old Testament books in the Catholic Bible are seven books not included in the Jewish and Protestant bibles and five additions to existing biblical books. They are known collectively as Deuterocanonical. Protestants call these the Apocrypha, which means "hidden books" in Greek. They include the Wisdom of Solomon, the Letter of Jeremiah, and 1 and 2 Maccabees, among others.

The Ten Commandments and Catholic Ethics

A succinct summary of Catholic ethics can be found in Psalm 34 in the Old Testament: "Turn from evil, and do good; seek peace and pursue it." Departing from evil for Christians means keeping the Ten Commandments, which the patriarch Moses received from God on Mount Sinai in the Jewish Bible. Doing good is due to practicing the four cardinal virtues of prudence, justice, fortitude, and temperance. These cardinal virtues were first put forth by the ancient Greek philosophers, and all other virtues derive from them.

The Ten Commandments are basic rules to live by for all Jews and Christians. No numbers are given to the commandments in the Old Testament. Augustine later divided and numbered them, and his listing is still followed by Catholics today. Other authors numbered them in different ways. For Catholics, each commandment has a broader scope than its literal meaning. For example, the first commandment forbids the worship of false gods. In Catholicism, this includes superstition, divination

The Epistles: Biblical Letters

Although the four Gospels are considered the central focus of the New Testament, most of this part of the Bible is taken up by twenty-one letters, also known as Epistles, written by the early Church's fathers. These are not letters as we think of them today, but more formal, lengthy writings directed to the early Christian congregations in the Mediterranean world founded by Paul and other apostles. Paul and the other epistle writers encourage, inspire, praise, and chastise their congregations in these letters. They also explain accepted Church beliefs and their own personal journeys of faith.

Paul is generally believed to have written most, if not all, of the first fourteen epistles, called the Pauline letters. Each letter is named after the people of the congregation or the person he is addressing. For example, Romans is named for the congregation in Rome and Ephesians for the congregation at Ephesus, a city in Greece.

In Paul's epistle to the Philippians, he expresses the joyous message of Christ. This excerpt is from the fourth and last chapter of Philippians, verses 4-7:

> **Rejoice in the Lord always. I will say it again: Rejoice! Let your gentleness be evident to all. The Lord is near. Do not be anxious about anything, but in everything, by prayer and petition, with thanksgiving, present your requests to God. And the peace of God, which transcends all understanding, will greet your hearts and your minds in Christ Jesus.**

The patriarch Moses carries the Ten Commandments, the laws he received directly from God. These commandments are still upheld today by the Catholic Church. This seventeenth-century painting is the work of Guido Reni.

(fortune telling), sacrilege (irreverence), and atheism. Although some Christians have criticized the Ten Commandments for their negativity and "shall nots," the Church points out that sin must be avoided so that virtue can be practiced. Under the four cardinal virtues described in the Bible's Book of Wisdom are many other human or natural virtues. Under justice, for example, are found piety, patriotism, honesty, and impartiality. The three supernatural or theological virtues that Paul writes about in I Corinthians are faith, hope, and charity. Through them, the soul is united to God in belief, expectation, and love. In Christian life, these three should reign supreme.

church tradition

Catholics see the Bible as the word of God. According to the principles of interpretation, Scripture has both a literal meaning and various spiritual meanings. The New Testament contains Jesus's teachings and thoughts and tells about such tenets of Catholic faith as the concepts of original sin, salvation, and the resurrection of Christ's body after death. But there are other tenets of faith that are not mentioned in the Bible. These include infant baptism and the structure of the Church's hierarchy. Both Jesus and Paul indirectly address the concept of the Trinity, but not in full detail. The Church bases many of these beliefs on the long tradition within the Church itself, which it claims goes back to the time of the apostles. Over time, these beliefs have become part of the core of the Roman Catholic faith.

The Apostolic succession

The arbiter, or final teacher and judge, of Catholic beliefs is the pope—the visible head of the Church—together with the bishops. Catholics believe that the pope is God's representative on earth, the successor of the apostle Peter. When the pope speaks *ex cathedra*, which in Latin literally means "from the chair," on matters of faith and morals, he is infallible. The bishops can likewise teach infallibly when gathered, with papal approval, in an ecumenical council. The tenet of faith that supports this belief is known as the apostolic succession. It refers to the unbroken line of popes from Saint Peter and the other apostles, who Catholics believe were chosen to lead the Church by Jesus himself, to today's pope. The commission that Jesus gave to Peter to "feed my lambs"(John 21:15), meaning his followers, is still considered the serious charge of the Church—to teach, to sanctify (purify), and to govern its members. The Church points to the papacy, the only earthly authority that has lasted for two thousand years, as a sign of God's divine blessing.

This doctrine of infallibility extends to the ecumenical or general councils that have been formed by the pope, and which are attended by all the bishops, to discuss and decide important issues of the Church. There have been twenty-one such councils held since 325. The last one, Vatican II, took place from 1962 to 1965.

concept of the Holy Trinity

In Roman Catholicism, God is the creator of all things. He is all-knowing and all-loving. He is also three persons in one—God the father; Jesus Christ, the son of God; and the Holy Spirit. These three form the Holy Trinity. According to Catholic doctrine Jesus the son was sent to earth to die as atonement for the sins of humankind and to establish a new religion that would be built around him, the Messiah who was foretold in the Old Testament. Jesus is the central focus of Roman Catholicism: it is "Christocentric." But it is the Holy Spirit who continues to work daily in the lives of Christians and the Church. The New Testament book the Acts of the Apostles reports that the Holy Spirit first appeared as tongues of fiery flame over the apostles' heads on Pentecost, fifty days after Jesus's resurrection from the dead. The Holy Spirit inspired the apostles to go out and preach the gospel of Jesus to the world.

veneration of the virgin mary and other saints

While only God is worshipped in the Roman Catholic Church, Catholics do pray to miraculously holy people of the past known as saints to intercede for them with God or Jesus. To be officially called a saint, a person must be canonized by the pope, a lengthy process that can take years, even centuries.

Saints are specially honored by Catholics. Statues and other images of saints are displayed in Catholic churches. Children are named for saints. Churches have been named for saints since the fourth century. Saints' feast days are celebrated in many Catholic countries. The most honored saint in the Church is the Virgin Mary, the mother of Jesus. One of the most important prayers in the Catholic Church, "Hail Mary," is addressed to her. Catholics in certain professions or situations pray to patron saints for special help or protection.

original sin and the promise of salvation

In Catholic theology, humans are fallen, sinful creatures. The origin of this sinful nature is explained in the biblical story of the Garden of Eden in Genesis, the first book of the Old Testament. Adam and Eve, the first man and woman, ate of the fruit from the Tree of the Knowledge of Good and Evil despite God's command not to do so. As a result of this act of disobedience, they were banished from the garden and began to suffer hard labor, pain, and death. Not until the birth of Jesus, which Christians believe was prophesied in the Old Testament, was there hope for the restoration of fallen human nature.

The Virgin Mary, mother of Jesus, is revered by Catholics around the world. This image of Mary and the infant Jesus is a key one in Catholic art.

patron saints

A saint is named a patron saint for a particular group of people either by tradition or election within the Church. A commission appointed by the Church examines a person's life for signs of sainthood, but only the pope can grant final official recognition. The reasons for the choices may be based on what a saint did in life or a special interest that he or she had. For example, Saint Francis of Assisi (about 1181–1226) was a great lover of nature and animals, and is therefore the patron saint of ecologists. Saint Patrick, who converted the Irish to Christianity in the fifth century, is the patron saint of Ireland. Saint Aloysius Gonzaga (1568–1591), who lived centuries before acquired immunodeficiency syndrome (AIDS), may seem an odd choice for the patron saint of that disease's caregivers and patients. However, Aloysius did care for plague victims in Rome, and he himself died of the plague at the age of twenty-three. He is also the patron saint of youth.

Here are just a few of the thousands of the Church's patron saints and whom they protect or what they help with:

Patron Saints of Nations

Saint Bridget	Sweden
Saint Denis	France
Saint George	England

Patron Saints of Trades and Professions

Saint Andrew	fishermen
Saint Damian	doctors
Saint Vitus	comedians

Patron Saints of Illnesses

Saint Benedict	kidney disease
Saint Cornelius	earaches
Saint Erasmus	abdominal pains

Jesus's sacrifice of his life on the cross washed away both original sin and personal sins and reopened the door to paradise after death (redemption).

Although redemption is a fact of Catholic belief, it is not granted automatically. Just as Adam and Eve had free will to accept or reject God, so do Catholics today. For Catholics, acceptance of Jesus Christ is the key to salvation. Non-Christians, who through no fault of their own do not accept Jesus, can be saved as well if they lead good lives.

A Life after Death

A person's soul, his or her spiritual being, does not die with the body at the moment of death, the Church teaches. The soul is immortal and leaves the body to be judged by God and sent to heaven, hell, or purgatory. Heaven is the destination for the souls of people who are in a state of grace. In heaven they bask for eternity in the vision of God. Hell is the netherworld, ruled by Satan, a fallen angel. This is where the souls of unrepentant people who lived evil lives go. In medieval times, hell was illustrated as a terrible place of fire, brimstone (sulfur), and agonizing physical pain. In modern times, the Church has chosen to play down the physical side of hell and emphasizes it as a place that is made unbearable for the sinner by the complete absence of God.

Purgatory is a place where imperfect but not completely sinful souls are purified through punishment. Unlike the residents of hell, those in purgatory know that one day when their penance is done, they will be admitted to heaven. Limbo is a comfortable place where infants who died unbaptized enjoy the fellowship of God without being able to see him. The existence of limbo is not an official tenet of the Catholic faith, but a probable opinion first put forth by theologians in the Middle Ages.

Ever since Jesus ascended into heaven, the Church has been expecting his return "to judge the living and the dead" (1 Peter 4:5 or the first epistle of Peter) as the Creed phrases it. "Behold, I am coming soon!" the book of Revelation (22:7) declares, bearing in mind that "with the Lord, a day is as a thousand years and a thousand years are like a day" (2 Peter 3:8). Jesus's return will be preceded by a period of great tribulation on earth, before he comes to reward or punish each individual according to his or her deeds.

Christian doctrine says that on the Day of Judgment, Jesus will return to earth and as a result all living people and all the dead will be sent to heaven or to hell. All souls that have already departed will be reunited with their resurrected bodies. The apostles thought the Day of Judgment could happen at any time, as did people living in the Middle Ages. Church doctrine does not specify a definite time for Jesus's Second Coming but urges all Catholics to be prepared for it.

three

ORGANIZATION AND STRUCTURE

The Roman Catholic Church has one of the most structured hierarchies of any of the world's major religious organizations. The Church's social organization is based on the New Testament classification of bishops, presbyters (or priests), and deacons; and on the political and legal systems of the Romans, who adopted Christianity in the fourth century.

The pope and the college of cardinals

The word *pope* is derived from the Latin word *papa*, meaning "father." The pope is seen as the father and head of the Church family. In that role, he is the ultimate authority and power in the Church. He decides Church policy, appoints cardinals and bishops, and teaches Catholics worldwide by encyclicals and other documents. The pope also meets with world leaders and has the power to discipline disobedient clergy and laypersons.

The pope has a huge support system that keeps him informed and aids him in carrying out his many duties. The cardinals, the highest-ranking clergymen after the pope, known collectively as the College of Cardinals or the Sacred College, elect the pope and are his main advisers. Cardinals are appointed by the pope from among the world's bishops. Most cardinals are bishops, and many head the administrative units of the Church called dioceses around the world. Others reside full-time in Rome and serve the pope in the Vatican. These are part of the Roman Curia, a vast administrative body with numerous departments and offices that assist him in the day-to-day operation of the Church. The Swiss Guard is the pope's personal army and has protected popes for centuries. Michelangelo designed their colorful uniforms. In January 2006, the Swiss Guard celebrated the five hundredth anniversary of its founding.

Electing a New Pope

When a pope dies, the College of Cardinals meets and elects a new pope, who is usually one of them. The process is a complicated one, full of age-old traditions. The cardinals gather in the Sistine Chapel to vote for the new pope. They fill out ballots called scrutinies and drop them into a gold cup on a table in front of the altar. The ballots are counted, and the man who receives two-thirds of the votes is declared pope. If no one achieves this number, the cardinals immediately vote again. If there is still no winner in a second round of voting, the scrutinies are mixed with chemicals and burned. (In earlier times, they were mixed with straw.) The black smoke that billows from the chimney tells the anxious crowd gathered outside in Saint Peter's Square that a pope has not yet been elected.

After a week of balloting, a simple majority will elect a new pope. When a pope is finally chosen, the scrutinies are burned with no chemicals. The white smoke that pours out of the chimney and the accompanying chiming of church bells tell the crowd that a pope has been chosen and the people cry out, *"Viva il papa!"* ("Long live the pope"). Since the pope's home is in Vatican City and the majority of cardinals are Italian, most popes have been Italian. John Paul II was the first non-Italian pope since 1523.

The Bishops and Their Dioceses

Although the pope is the Church's head, it is the Church's bishops— some of whom are cardinals—who are the hands that carry out much

of his work. Most bishops, before they are appointed by the pope and consecrated, are priests. Each bishop is in charge of a diocese, the basic administrative unit of the Church. (The largest dioceses are often overseen by cardinals.) The diocese is further divided into a number of parishes, Catholic communities centered around a church. The bishop appoints pastors, priests who oversee and run each parish. Bishops also have the power to initiate new priests through the sacrament of holy orders and have the power to remove priests and other clergy from a parish or position for disobedience or improper

Bishop Edward Egan is installed as archbishop of New York in a Mass at Saint Patrick's Cathedral in June 2000. Note the crosier he wields, a symbol of the power and authority of bishops in the Church.

behavior. Only the pope, however, can laicize a priest, return him to lay status, and cut his ties to his diocese.

In a bishop's administrative duties, he is usually assisted by a vicar-general, a chancellor, and lesser officials. In a large diocese, the bishop may be given the title archbishop and have deputy bishops assisting him.

The Synod of Bishops is a representative consulting body established by Pope Paul VI in 1965. It met for the first time in Vatican City in 1967. There have been thirteen synods or general assemblies to date; the latest took place in October 2005.

vatican city—The pope's Home and catholic Headquarters

Despite its name, Vatican City is not a city but a tiny independent country of about 109 acres (44 hectares) located in the heart of Rome. Yet the Vatican's importance is far greater that its physical size might indicate. From this small place, a worldwide Church is governed and run by about four thousand employees who assist the pope and live mostly outside the Vatican. The entire population of Vatican City is only about one thousand.

The Vatican is dominated by the Apostolic Palace, commonly called the Pope's Palace, where the pope resides. This imposing building has more than 1,400 rooms, 20 courtyards, and close to 1,000 flights of stairs. The pope lives on the top floor. Many of his staff stay in apartments on other floors.

The other major architectural landmark of the Vatican is Saint Peter's Basilica, the central cathedral and the largest church building in the world. It has fifty altars, including the High Altar, where the pope regularly celebrates Mass. There are numerous chapels and more than four hundred statues. Under the basilica is the tomb of Emperor Constantine.

Vatican City has no restaurants, hotels, or hospitals, and the only school is devoted to the making of mosaics, which are created and sold there. It does have a supermarket, a pharmacy, a world-famous library, and a post office that sells its own postage stamps. The Vatican postal system is one of the world's most efficient and handles more items each year per resident than any other postal system in the world. Much of this mail consists of postcards mailed by tourists. The Vatican also has its own daily newspaper and radio and television stations that broadcast around the world.

The Vatican, a nation within a nation, is the geographical heart and soul of the Roman Catholic Church.

pastors and other priests

The pastor in charge of a parish is the spiritual leader of all those Catholics within his parish, who are called the parishioners. There are two kinds of parishes. A territorial parish is defined by a geographic area and includes all Catholics who live within its boundaries. A national parish is based on ethnicity and includes all Catholics who are members of a particular ethnic group, regardless of what territorial parish they live in. Since many Catholics, especially in the United States, move from the ethnic neighborhoods of the cities to more multicultural suburbs, the number of national parishes is rapidly declining.

Many pastors are assisted by associate or assistant pastors, who are usually also priests. To become a priest, a man must attend a school for religious training called a seminary for four to six years. Once they are ordained through the sacrament of holy orders, priests may celebrate the Mass (Eucharist), the most important liturgical rite and sacrament of the Catholic Church; administer other sacraments; preach; and perform various duties. Not all priests are assigned to serve in a parish. Many serve as educators and administrators in Catholic schools, colleges, and universities; work in the offices of bishops; or serve in other Catholic institutions including hospitals and charities. Priests, depending on the order they belong to, owe their immediate allegiance and obedience to a bishop, the head of their order, or the pope. The pope, however, is the highest superior of all.

monks and nuns

Not all members of the religious community are ordained as priests and bishops and work in the wider world. Those who choose the monastic life live in monasteries or convents. While monks and other monastic males can be priests, many are not ordained and are called brothers. All Catholic monastics take vows of chastity, poverty, and obedience. Monks who are not priests cannot celebrate the Eucharist or perform other sacraments. Their lives are devoted to manual work, prayer, and study.

There are two basic kinds of monastics—active, who do some form of service, often outside the monastery; and contemplative, who devote almost all their time to prayer and work in a cloister, a secluded monastery. The members of cenobitic orders live a completely communal life, interacting regularly with the other religious persons, bound by monastic vows, in the community. Cenobites can be either

Like priests and monks, the number of nuns in the United States is shrinking. The average age of the 73,000 nuns in the United States today is 69. As these women retire or die, there are few new nuns to replace them. Note the rosary beads, a praying tool, that this nun is wearing.

active or contemplative. Members of eremitic orders live lives of contemplative solitude. Although they come together at special times as a community, much of their time is spent alone in prayer and study in individual rooms known as cells. Widespread in the early centuries of the Church, relatively few eremitic monasteries are left today.
Women in the Catholic Church are not admitted to the priesthood. They can become nuns, female monastics, and can be either cenobites or eremites. They live communally in convents. Many nuns are teachers, hospital workers, or charity workers. Others, like the Carmelites and Poor Clares, are cloistered contemplatives.

The Laity

The laity are those members of the Catholic Church who are not members of the clergy or religious life. Traditionally, laypersons are called to be active witnesses to the faith in the world by leading good, Christian lives and setting an example for others to follow. Since Vatican II, laypeople have been encouraged to take a more active part in worship, liturgy, and evangelization (converting others to Catholicism). Today laypeople assist with Holy Communion, read from Scripture during services, teach Sunday school, and serve on parish councils and boards.

As the number of priests has dwindled in the past several decades, more laymen are being ordained permanent deacons, a form of clergy. They assist priests in celebrating Mass, preach from the pulpit, and can witness marriages, perform baptisms, officiate at funerals, and help the sick and the shut-in of the parish. (These men are not to be confused with transitional deacons, men who are ordained as deacons as a step toward eventual priesthood.) Other laypeople have become associates (called oblates and tertiaries) of religious orders. These people can, if they choose, take a type of promise of chastity, obedience, and poverty, adjusted to their style of life. They cultivate the order's spirituality and may also work faithfully for its mission, particularly in the areas of education and charity.

The Roman Catholic Church is a vast and complex organization with many members. Each member has a role to play in keeping the body whole and healthy.

TRADITIONS, CUSTOMS, AND RITES

The rites and liturgy of the Roman Catholic church reflect a rich heritage two thousand years old. Every feature of these customs, from the priest's vestments (garments) to the incense that fills the air of the sanctuary (the part of the church around the altar) on high holy days, is rich in symbolism and meaning.

The Mass and the Eucharist

The Mass is a sacrificial religious rite that re-creates and celebrates the death and resurrection of Jesus through the Eucharist, the sacrament of Holy Communion. Other Christians also observe Holy Communion and call it "the Lord's supper." Jesus gave his apostles the eucharistic rite just before he was arrested and crucified, saying, "Do this in remembrance of me" (Luke 22:19). The eucharistic Mass is the heart of Catholic worship and liturgy. Vatican II called the Eucharist "the source and summit of the Christian life." It reminds Catholics of the great debt that they owe their savior. It is so critical to Catholic life that every Catholic is required to attend Mass each Sunday, the Lord's Day. Most churches offer Mass daily and on Saturday evening for those who cannot attend on Sunday morning.

The Mass is divided into two parts. The first half, called the liturgy of the word, consists of hymns, prayers, scriptural readings from the Old and New Testaments (called the epistle

The elements of bread and wine are ready to be distributed during Holy Communion, one of the seven sacraments of the Roman Catholic Church. Through the mystery of transubstantiation they are converted into the body and blood of Jesus.

and the gospel), and a homily or sermon from the celebrant—the priest celebrating the Mass. The eucharistic liturgy follows. At the altar, the celebrant offers gifts of bread and wine to God as he re-creates the Last Supper that Jesus shared with his disciples the day before he died. The priest, taking on the role of Jesus, changes the bread and wine into the body and blood of Christ with words and gestures. This change is not symbolic, as in Protestant churches, but is believed to actually take place through the mystery of transubstantiation. "Our gifts of bread and wine are changed by Christ from being symbols of ourselves and our self-giving to being Christ himself and his self-giving," explains Catholic writer Ron Hansen. "They are no longer things; they are God."

The celebrant eats the "transubstantiated" bread and drinks the wine and then offers the bread to the congregants, who usually come to the altar rail to receive it in the part of Mass called Holy Communion. While the bread can be fashioned in any form, it must be made only of water and wheat flour. It is usually served as a round wafer-thin piece of unleavened bread called a host. Sacramental wine can also be served at the discretion of the pastor. Because the bread is Christ's body and the wine is Christ's blood, only Catholics whose souls are free of unconfessed, unforgiven sins can receive it. As a general rule, Church law does not permit non-Catholic Christians to receive Communion.

After Holy Communion is received, the Mass ends in prayer and songs of thanksgiving.

THE SEVEN SACRAMENTS

Holy Communion (the Eucharist) is one of the seven sacraments of the Catholic Church. A sacrament is an outward sign in words and gestures that communicates inward grace, God's freely given and unmerited love. Most sacraments mark a stage of growth or change in the individual recipient's relationship to Jesus and the Church. These are the other six sacraments:

Baptism

Baptism takes place shortly after a Catholic is born (although adult converts may also be baptized). In this rite the individual is believed to be cleansed of original sin and, filled with grace and the Holy Spirit, to enter into a personal relationship with Jesus. Baptism can be performed as a separate service in the Catholic Church. The infant or child is accompanied to the altar by his or her parents and godparents. The godparents are chosen by the parents as mentors for the child. If anything should happen to the parents, the godparents are responsible for the child's religious upbringing. The family joins the priest at the baptismal font, a basin filled with holy water, which has been blessed by the priest. The priest pours the holy water over the infant's forehead, and he anoints him or her with holy oil as a symbol of cleansing the child of sin and his or her rebirth into a new life in Christ. Although baptism transforms the soul of the recipient, an infant is too young to comprehend this. The parents and godparents speak for her or him during the baptismal service.

Confirmation

When the baptized child reaches a certain maturity, he or she receives the sacrament of confirmation, which grants a permanent grace on the soul and completes the process of induction (admission into the Church) begun by baptism. The child receives instruction in the teachings of Jesus and the Church during confirmation classes. When these classes end, he or she is ready to be confirmed and made a full member of the Church.

The sacrament of confirmation is usually administrated by the bishop of the diocese. The bishop extends his hand over each confirmand, a sign of the coming of the Holy Spirit to him or her. He also makes the sign of the cross on the person's forehead with a special holy oil called chrism. As another sign of change, the confirmand may take a second middle name. This confirmation name is the name of a saint or a Christian mystery or a virtue, such as Earnest, Constance, or Grace.

Penance

Although original sin has been washed away at baptism, all people continue to sin during their lives. These personal sins must be confessed, and the sinner must ask for forgiveness to remain in God's good graces. The sacrament of penance, also called reconciliation or confession, is a public demonstration of this act of confession and repentance, in which God absolves (forgives) sins through his representative, the priest. Each church has its own weekly hours of confession. Confessional booths are located on the sides of the sanctuary. During this time, the priest sits in the darkened booth. When a penitent enters, the priest opens a screen to speak to the person. Neither penitent nor priest can see each other clearly. This is to keep anonymity in the confessional. The penitent recites the sins that he or she has committed since the last time of confession and expresses repentance for them. The priest then administers absolution and gives the person a penance, usually a number of prayers to recite. The penitent goes to the altar rail to kneel and perform the penance. The option of face-to-face confession was introduced after Vatican II, and some penitents prefer it.

Some Catholics have questioned the role of penance in the Church. They ask why a person should have to confess to a priest and not directly to God. Vatican II reconsidered the nature of penance, emphasizing the effect it produces of reconciliation with God and

This happy couple has just given each other the sacrament of matrimony. Catholic marriage cannot be dissolved, and a married Catholic can only marry again when a spouse dies or the Church grants the couple an annulment.

with the Church. Catholics are still required to go to confession a minimum of once a year and are encouraged to go more frequently as a means of spiritual growth. Frequent confession of one's sins directly to God in prayer is also encouraged, especially by using a traditional memorized formula called the Act of Contrition.

Matrimony

Matrimony, or marriage, is considered a sacramental joining of the souls of a baptized man and woman who enter into this union before the Church. The central purposes of matrimony are unity in love and the procreation of children. It is the only sacrament that is not ministered, but rather witnessed, by the officiating priest. The bride and the groom give the sacrament to each other as they come together in sacred partnership. In the marriage vows, the two people promise to be faithful to each other and raise any children they have in the Catholic Church. The marriage ceremony can be incorporated into a Mass.

Because marriage is a sacrament, it cannot be dissolved. The Church does not recognize divorce. A Catholic may marry again only if his or her spouse dies or if the Church grants the couple an annulment. An annulment is a formal declaration, based on the investigation of an ecclesiastical tribunal, that no true marriage ever occurred. "Mixed marriages," in which one's partner is a non-Catholic Christian, are allowed as long as the couple agrees to raise any children they have in the Catholic faith. Marriage to a non-baptized partner is also allowed under similar circumstances.

Holy Orders

The sacrament of holy orders is the initiation of men into the clerical state as deacons, priests, or bishops. It is one of only three sacraments that can be ministered just once. The other two are baptism and confirmation. These three sacraments are said to imprint a permanent character on the soul. The minister of holy orders must be a bishop. This sacrament has three grades: the lowest is the deaconate (which must precede the priesthood); the middle grade is the ordinary priesthood; and the highest is the episcopacy, called "the fullness of the priesthood," reserved for bishops. During ordination, the priest-to-be takes vows of chastity and obedience to the bishop. The new priest also celebrates Mass during the ordination and is later assigned to a parish or to another position within the diocese or his order.

The Anointing of the Sick

Until Vatican II, this sacrament was known as Extreme Unction, a name that led many Catholics to believe it was ministered only to those who were near death from illness or advanced age. The name change was meant to stress that the sacrament is for anyone who is seriously ill and not just for the dying. The emphasis now is on the healing, comfort, and forgiveness that anointing of the sick can bring and not on the possibility of death. The priest rubs holy oil onto the sick person's head, hands, and feet, then prays for and blesses the individual. The action of the anointing may be repeated later for the same person if he or she does not improve.

"At the center of each sacrament, is an act of worship;" writes Catholic author Mary Gordon, "each sacrament involves the role of the individual in the worshipping community, a community whose very reason for its existence is the presence in it of God. It is the relationship between the lived life and the eternal one that makes up the form of every sacrament."

sacramentals

Besides the seven sacraments, there are other rites or objects in the Catholic Church called sacramentals whose purpose is to prepare for and extend the blessings brought by the sacraments. Sacramentals often honor and elevate to a spiritual level the ordinary and everyday activities of life that are often taken for granted. In agricultural societies that might be the blessing of a harvest. When a new Catholic school or university is built, it is consecrated and blessed in a special ceremony. Many churches in the United States and elsewhere celebrate a yearly blessing of the animals, in which families bring their pets and farm animals to the church grounds for a blessing from the pastor. These events are often accompanied by festivities.

prayers, devotions, and other catholic customs

Prayer is a cornerstone of Roman Catholicism. It typically consists of a person talking to God. Some of the purposes of prayer are to worship God, to thank him, or to ask for his help or guidance. Catholics pray in church during Mass and other religious services; before meals, when they say grace; and often before bedtime or upon waking in the morning. Prayer vigils are held in churches during certain holy days or at other special times. Parishioners sign up for a certain hour, night or day, to pray in the church sanctuary or at home for a particular purpose, such as world peace. Priests are required to read from the Divine Office, a daily set of prayers and scriptural readings. Many churches hold regular prayer and healing services where church members raise up to God in their prayers the needs of the sick and the impoverished of the parish.

Rosary beads are a special form of prayer and devotion. Each bead on the string represents a prayer and is used as a memory aid. The large beads represent the Lord's Prayer, also known as the Our Father, and the doxology, a liturgical formula of praise to God. The small beads represent the prayer known as the Hail Mary. A crucifix attached to the beads represents the Apostles' Creed prayer. To say the complete rosary consists of reciting prayers around the string of beads three times and meditating on certain mysteries of the faith, significant events in the lives of Jesus and the Virgin Mary.

Many Catholic churches have holy or votive candles in the sanctuary near the altar. A person puts some money into a box and lights a candle for a friend or family member, often someone who is sick or facing some other problem.

Another Church custom is to bless oneself with holy water contained in a small dish when entering a church. The person uses the fingers they dipped in the water to form the sign of the cross on their forehead and chest. Another sign of respect in a church is to kneel on one knee when crossing in front of the altar. This shows reverence for both the altar and the tabernacle, the ornamental receptacle on the altar that contains the Holy Eucharist.

Fasting, abstaining from eating and drinking, is an important part of Catholic life, even though the rules have been much relaxed since Vatican Council II. For example, the fast before Holy Communion has been reduced to one hour. Friday, the day on which Jesus died, is to be a day of penance for Catholics according to current Church law, although in the United States some other form of penance than abstinence from meat may be chosen by the individual. Many Catholics still give up eating certain foods, such as desserts, during Lent—the forty days before Easter—a traditional time of reflection and penance. Fasting on Ash Wednesday and Good Friday, important days in the Catholic calendar, and abstinence from meat on the Fridays of Lent are required today.

Relics—Holy objects

Relics are parts of the body, such as hair or bones, or personal possessions of Jesus or a saint of the Church. Relics are considered holy objects and are traditionally believed to have miracles associated with them. The occasional liquefaction of the coagulated blood of the martyr Saint Januarius in Naples, Italy, has been one of the most frequently investigated of such phenomena. Today the Church's official policy about relics is that they are worthy of veneration because of their connection with the holy bodies of the saints.

The most precious relics are those associated with Jesus, such as the veil of Saint Veronica, said to be used to wipe Jesus's face on the way to his crucifixion, and the Shroud of Turin. According to tradition, every Catholic church altar is supposed to contain one relic as a blessing. This tradition dates to the earliest days of the Church in Rome, when Mass was celebrated in secrecy over the graves of martyrs.

Some relics are deposited in shrines, to which devout Christians make pilgrimages. One of the most famous of these shrines is in Canterbury, England, and honors the relics of Saint Thomas à Beckett, murdered on the orders of King Henry II. It has been a popular pilgrims' destination since medieval times and inspired English author Geoffrey Chaucer to write The *Canterbury Tales*.

Holy Days of Obligation

The Church has designated six holy days as days of obligation when Catholics in the United States are required to attend Mass. These days may differ slightly from nation to nation because local bishops determine them. In Mexico, for example, the feast of Our Lady of Guadalupe (December 12) is a holy day of obligation. Easter, the day of Christ's resurrection, is not included because it always falls on a Sunday when Catholics must attend Mass anyway. In America, these six days are: the Feast of Mary, mother of God (January 1); the Ascension, when Jesus went to heaven (Thursday of the sixth week after Easter); the Assumption of the Blessed Virgin Mary, when the body of Mary was taken to heaven by angels to be with Jesus (August 15); All Saints' Day (November 1); the Immaculate Conception, referring to Mary's birth which was free of original sin (December 8); and the Nativity, or birth of Jesus, commonly known as Christmas (December 25). In 1991 the U.S. Conference of Bishops ruled that when January 1, August

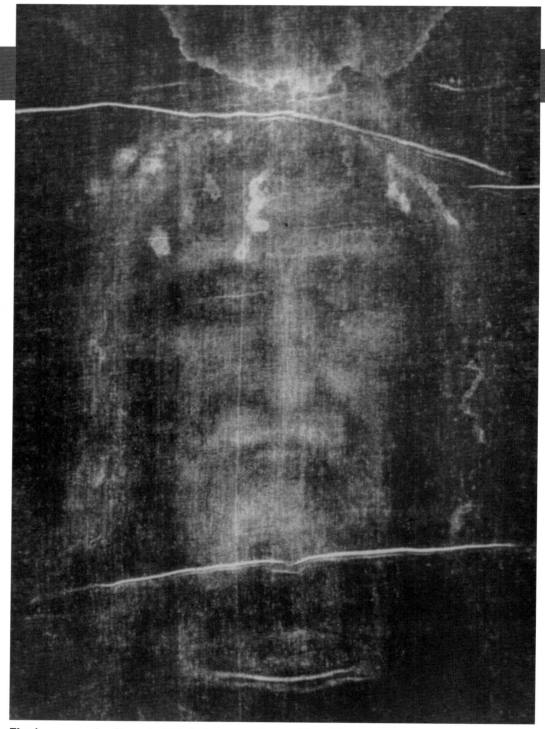

The image on the Shroud of Turin is generally considered by Catholics to be the face of Jesus Christ. They believe the shroud held Jesus's body in the tomb. Modern scientific technology confirms many aspects of the shroud's age and location.

the shroud of turin

The most famous and controversial relic in Catholicism, the Shroud of Turin is supposedly the garment in which Jesus's body was wrapped in his tomb before his resurrection. The cloth bears the life-size impression of a man whom some believe was whipped and crucified and had borne a crown of thorns.

The shroud's history is as intriguing as its alleged origins. It or a similar cloth was first recorded in Asia Minor in the sixth century. It was brought to Constantinople but disappeared and was probably stolen in the thirteenth century. A little over a century later, it turned up in France and was partially burned in a fire in 1532. In 1578 it was brought to a chapel in Turin, Italy, where it has mostly remained ever since.

In 1978 a team of more than forty scientists was allowed to closely examine and test the shroud to determine its authenticity. The results were stunning. The shroud was found to contain amounts of pollen and mites—tiny insects— that could only have come from the area of the Dead Sea in Israel. The bloodstains were proved to come from the blood of a human male. Microscopic bits of limestone dust on the shroud were similar to that found in the tombs of Jerusalem. Perhaps most convincing of all was the computer imaging that detected an object over the right eye of the impressed face. The image was that of a Roman coin from Palestine about 29 B.C.E. It was customary at that time to put coins over the eyes of the dead. Ten years later, in 1988, a carbon 14 test showed that the shroud was a medieval cloth, but since then this test has been challenged by many scientists.

On his death in 1983, King Umberto II of Italy willed the Shroud of Turin to the Vatican. On September 5, 1995, the papal custodian of the holy shroud declared the image on the shroud to be that of Jesus Christ and "no one else." Many devout Catholics have called the shroud the "Fifth Gospel," a miraculous testament to the death and divinity of Jesus.

15, and November 1 fall on a Saturday or Monday, Catholics are not required to attend Mass.

The observance of christmas and easter

Christmas, commemorating the birth of Jesus Christ, is the second-most important religious holiday in the Church calendar. The word *Christmas* comes from the Old English phrase *Cristes maesse*, meaning "Mass of Christ." Catholics prepare for Christmas with the season of Advent, the four weeks before Christmas. Churches and homes display Advent wreathes made of evergreen boughs and holding four candles, one for each week of Advent. One candle is lit by parishioners or family members each week, and a fifth candle—symbolizing Jesus—is added to the wreath on Christmas Day.

Churches honor the birth of Jesus with special decorations which may include a Christmas tree with the star of Bethlehem on top and a crèche—a nativity scene—with figures of Mary, baby Jesus, Joseph, the shepherds, animals, and the Three Wise Men or Magi who brought gifts for the infant. Some churches sponsor living nativities with real people and animals.

On Christmas Eve many Catholics attend a special Midnight Mass with a full procession of clergy and altar boys and a choir singing Christmas carols. It is one of the most colorful services of the Church year. The Christmas season continues with Epiphany, which celebrates the coming of the Three Wise Men or Magi to the child's birthplace in Bethlehem, and it concludes with the feast day of the Baptism of the Lord in early January.

Easter Sunday, which commemorates the day of Jesus's resurrection (his rising from the dead), is the most important Church holy day. It is preceded by the forty days (not counting Sundays) of Lent, a period of reflection and penance. The period of Lent corresponds to the forty days that Jesus spent praying and fasting in the wilderness before he began to teach publicly. Lent begins with Ash Wednesday, a day when Catholics attend Mass and have a priest make a cross on their foreheads with ashes to remind them of their mortality.

Holy Week is the seven-day period preceding Easter. It begins on Palm (Passion) Sunday, which marks the day when Jesus entered Jerusalem to celebrate the Jewish Passover with his disciples. Palm leaves, which the people of Jerusalem threw before Jesus to welcome and praise him, are distributed at the beginning of the service. Holy, or Maundy, Thursday honors the day that Jesus held the Last Supper with his disciples and was later arrested and imprisoned. Catholic churches hold special Masses. During the service, the priest may wash the feet of twelve parishioners to commemorate Jesus's washing the feet of his twelve disciples. On Good Friday, the day Jesus was crucified and died, no Mass is celebrated. It is a solemn time of prayer, reflection, and mourning. Holy Saturday is a day of waiting and vigil for the risen Christ to appear. The celebration of the Easter Vigil takes place at midnight, or at least after dark. The baptism of new members is held at this vigil, a tradition from the Church's earliest days. The Easter Vigil is the most important event of the entire liturgical year. It includes ceremonies of fire, light, and water, as well as many biblical readings.

In many churches in the United States, outdoor dawn services have become popular on Easter morning. The rising sun is seen by worshippers as a dramatic symbol of Jesus's resurrection. The Easter season reaches a peak on Ascension Day, which ends the forty-day period during which the resurrected Jesus reappeared to his disciples and other followers and marks Jesus's rising into heaven. The season comes to a formal end ten days later on Pentecost Sunday, which marks the descent of the Holy Spirit upon the apostles, who then went forth to preach and to build the foundation of the Christian Church.

five

THE EASTERN ORTHODOX CHURCH

The word *orthodox* comes from a greek word meaning "right believing."

The Eastern Orthodox Church and its 174 million worldwide followers pride themselves on remaining true to the traditions of the early Christian Church and being governed by bishops who are successors of the apostles.

organization

In a sense, there is not one Orthodox Church, but many. The Eastern Orthodox Church is composed of a fellowship of churches, mostly defined by the nation or region in which they exist. The churches are called autocephalous, meaning that they are independent, led by their own archbishops, who are also known as patriarchs or metropolitans. While the patriarchs are known as the heads of their churches, they do not have exclusive authority over them. Most Orthodox churches are also governed by a Holy Synod, a group of bishops and laypersons. The patriarch presides over the synod, but has limited power over it.

The patriarchate, the spiritual community over which a patriarch rules, is ranked in importance not by how many people belong to it, but by historical importance. The patriarch of Constantinople presides over one of the oldest Orthodox congregations. Today, Constantinople is the Turkish city of Istanbul, which is mostly Muslim, and the patriarch's congregation is a small one. The other historic

Mount Athos—The Republic of Monasteries

In northern Greece, on the southern tip of a peninsula extending into the Aegean Sea, there exists one of the most unusual religious communities on earth. There, at Mount Athos, there are more than 20 Orthodox monastic communities populated by more than 1,000 monks within about 30 square miles (78 square kilometers). The first monastery was established by Athanasios the Athonite under the Rule of Saint Basil about 963. By 1050 there were 7,000 monks. As the community grew and new monasteries developed, they were left to govern themselves by the Byzantine and then the Ottoman empires.

In 1822 Turkish soldiers attacked Athos, murdering many monks and looting the monasteries. The community survived and came under Greek rule in 1912. In 1927 the Greek government declared Mount Athos a theocratic republic (governed by divine guidance) ruled by the Patriarch of Constantinople. Monastic life declined steadily from then into the 1960s and experienced a revival in the mid-1970s. At present, it seems to be attracting many new members.

Aside from its spiritual importance, Mount Athos has one of the largest collections of Christian art in the world, which includes about 18,000 portable icons (religious paintings), as well as many murals and miniatures.

patriarchates in descending order of importance are in Alexandria, Egypt; Damascus, Syria; and Jerusalem. The modern countries that belong to the Eastern Orthodox Church include Russia, Georgia, Serbia, Romania, and Bulgaria. The Russian Orthodox Church is the largest of all the Orthodox Churches. There are also Orthodox Churches on the island of Cyprus; in Athens, Greece; and in Tirana, Albania. Smaller, less significant churches are found in Poland, the Czech Republic, and Slovakia. Although many of these national churches have members in the United States, an Orthodox Church of America was not established until 1970. Its goal is to unify all Orthodox churches in the United States and Canada into one territorial community.

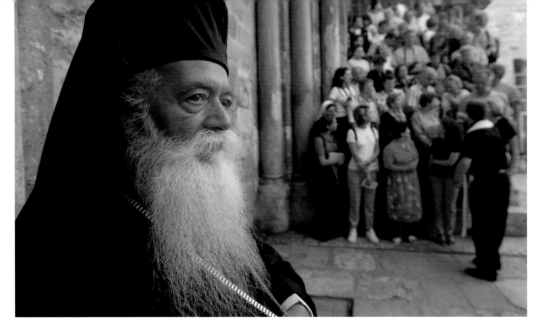

A Greek Orthodox priest sits outside the Church of the Holy Sepulchre in Jerusalem undisturbed by a group of nearby tourists. Unlike Catholic priests, Orthodox priests may marry before being ordained and are encouraged to do so. Orthodox bishops, however, are only elected from widowed or unmarried priests.

Beliefs and Tenets

The Eastern Orthodox Church follows much of the same Christian doctrine as does Roman Catholicism, but there are a few striking differences. Orthodox Christians do not recognize the supreme authority of the pope, nor do they believe that he, or any church leader, is infallible, a main tenet of the Roman Catholic Church.

The other central difference involves the concept of the Holy Trinity. The Nicene-Constantinopolitan Creed, decreed by the First Council of Constantinople in 381, which the Eastern Orthodox follow, states that the Holy Spirit "proceeds from the Father." Roman Catholics and many Protestants use a form of that creed that states the Holy Spirit "proceeds from the Father *and the Son*," Jesus Christ. This is known as "the filioque" in Christian theology.

Clergy

The three main orders in the Eastern Orthodox Church are bishops, priests, and deacons. Orthodox priests, unlike their Catholic counterparts, are strongly encouraged to marry, but only before they are ordained. Bishops are elected from among unmarried, monastic, or widowed priests, and they may not marry. Monastic priests must also be unmarried and live a communal life in monasteries, much as Catholic monks do. There are also female religious, or nuns, in the Orthodox Church. Deacons, who may marry as well only before being ordained, assist priests, as do subdeacons and readers.

customs and rites

The central liturgical rite of the Orthodox Church, equivalent to the Catholic Mass, is the Divine Liturgy. The celebration of the Eucharist is the focus of the ceremony, but it is celebrated much less regularly than the Catholic Mass. The entire service is sung or chanted by the priest and the congregation, and there is a procession of clergy. Both elements of Holy Communion are always served at the same time—bread and wine, usually on a spoon. Sometimes the host is dipped into the wine in a process called intinction.

The mystery and majesty of the early Christian Church is dramatically captured in the Orthodox service and the layout of the sanctuary. The altar is placed in the middle of the sanctuary, not at one end, and a partition or screen called an iconostasis separates the sanctuary and the congregation. This screen is covered with icons, and congregants peer through doorways in the screen to see the priest performing the service.

The Orthodox Church recognizes the same six other sacraments that the Catholic Church does, but there is no authority to limit the sacraments to these seven. There are also differences in the way the sacraments are administered. Orthodox baptism consists of totally immersing the person or child being baptized in water three times. When the ceremony has ended, the baptized person is immediately confirmed, to seal him or her with the Holy Spirit. Confirmation, also

These Orthodox nuns are celebrating during the midnight Easter liturgy in a Romanian monastery. Orthodox churches, following the old Julian calendar, usually celebrate Easter after Western Christians do.

icons—images of mystical power

The mysticism that is a central feature of the Eastern Orthodox faith is best displayed in its icons. These small painted objects mean much more to believers than the representations of Jesus, God, the Virgin Mary, and the saints. They make real the figure or mystery of faith that is represented.

The first known icons were created in the fifth century, although few examples survive from earlier than the tenth century. Icons hang in churches and other religious buildings, are carried in religious processions, and have an honored place in homes. In earlier centuries they were carried into battle on poles to protect Christian soldiers.

While these stylized, brilliantly colored paintings are regarded as a high form of art, few of the artists who created them over the centuries are known by name. The most celebrated Russian iconographer was the monk Andrey Rublyov (about 1360 to about 1430), who was recently canonized by the Moscow patriarchate. His icon of the Trinity is perhaps the most artistically beautiful and richly symbolic ever made.

called Chrismation, is performed by a priest, not a bishop, as is the norm in Catholicism. Divorce is permitted in the Orthodox Church and people may remarry, although most churches allow a maximum of three marriages for one person.

orthodox-catholic relations

The first serious conflict between the Eastern and Western churches occurred in the second century C.E., and many temporary schisms preceded the final break in 1054. For nearly a thousand years, there was little dialogue between the Eastern Orthodox Church and the

Roman Catholic Church. The attempts made at reconciliation by the several church councils, primarily the Council of Lyons (1274) and the Council of Florence (1445), failed. Meaningful dialogue did not come until the twentieth century. In 1948 Orthodox churches joined the growing ecumenical movement and became members of the World Council of Churches, formed that same year. In 1964 the first meeting of a pope and a patriarch of Constantinople since 1439 took place in Jerusalem between Pope Paul VI and Constantinople patriarch Athenagoras. The following year the two religious leaders removed the excommunication that certain officials of each church had placed on the other in 1054.

Pope John Paul II made reconciliation with the Orthodox Church a goal of his papacy. Although the dialogue progressed during his reign, there is no indication that the two Churches will reunite anytime soon. Many Orthodox patriarchs, priests, monks, and laypeople still take very seriously the ancient suspicion that they have inherited of "the Latins." Then there is the issue of the pope's authority and infallibility, which no one expects the Catholic Church to compromise.

Besides the Eastern Orthodox churches, there are also numerous Eastern Catholic churches in full contact with the papacy. They have their own liturgies and religious customs; some of them (those of the Byzantine Rite, the liturgy of the Mass celebrated in Constantinople centuries earlier) are identical with Eastern Orthodox ones. The biggest Byzantine Rite Catholic Church is in Ukraine. An important non-Byzantine Catholic Eastern Rite is the Chaldean Church of Iraq.

SIX

THE CATHOLIC CHURCH TODAY

The crowd that gathered in saint peter's square in vatican city near dusk on April 19, 2005, was restless and confused. The smoke that rose from the chimney of the Sistine Chapel in Saint Peter's Basilica did not look white. White smoke was a sign that the College of Cardinals had elected a new pope. But then the bells of the basilica began to ring, and with that joyful sound the crowd knew that the cardinals had reached their decision. The only question that remained was who was this new pope?

As the crowd continued to swell, a cardinal appeared on the balcony of the basilica to announce that Cardinal Joseph Ratzinger had become Pope Benedict XVI. Then the new seventy-eight-year-old pope, wearing the red cape of the papacy, appeared, waving at the crowd below as it chanted "Benedict! Benedict!"

The two-hundred-sixty-fifth pope had been chosen. His election had been one of the shortest in one hundred years. He is the first German pope in nearly one thousand years and the oldest pope elected since 1730. While he is well liked by his peers, Pope Benedict XVI will need all his resources to live up to the expectations created by his predecessors—one of the most popular popes in modern times—John Paul II.

The Roman Catholic Church and its new pope face many challenges. Some say the Church's very survival is in question. Others look to its two-thousand-year history and disregard such a

pope Benedict xvi

At age five, Joseph Ratzinger had already set his sights on one day becoming a cardinal. In the end, he would surpass that ambition and become pope.

He was born on April 16, 1927, in Marktl am Inn in southern Germany. His father was a policeman and a devout Catholic. When Joseph was six, the National Socialist Party, the Nazis, came to power under their leader, Adolph Hitler. Although the Ratzingers were opposed to Hitler's dictatorship, their son was forced to join the Hitler Youth at age fourteen. He was soon dismissed when he expressed his desire to become a priest. In 1943, in the midst of World War II, Ratzinger was drafted to work in an anti-aircraft unit. Later, he was drafted into the army and deserted at the war's end. He returned to the seminary after the war and was ordained a priest in 1951, at the same time as his brother Georg. His keen intellect and ability to articulate Catholic doctrine and his own faith made Ratzinger a popular lecturer at Bonn University beginning in 1959. An adviser to the Vatican II, he was made archbishop of Munich in 1977 and was elevated to cardinal three months later by Pope Paul VI. A favorite of Pope John Paul II, Ratzinger was summoned by him to Rome in 1981 to head the Congregation for the Doctrine of the Faith. In that role, Ratzinger was a defender of Catholic doctrine and a harsh critic of those who strayed from it, including his former friend German theologian Hans Küng. His critics called Cardinal Ratzinger "God's Rottweiler," and his supporters referred to him affectionately as "the German Shepherd."

Elected pope by the College of Cardinals on April 19, 2005, Pope Benedict XVI may yet surprise his critics by being more tolerant and reform-minded than they expected. "He has a very strong personality, but not a hard one," says Monsignor Erwin Gatz, "and when one is strong, one can also be tolerant." Whichever path the new pope chooses, it will have an immense impact on the future of the Roman Catholic Church.

pessimistic point of view. Yet few will deny that the Church in recent years has been under siege as it has rarely been before. Sexual abuse scandals, financial setbacks, and a growing shortage of priests and other religious are taking their toll.

The Sexual Abuse Scandal

The frequency of sexual misconduct among Catholic priests is, according to experts, no greater than the frequency among the clergy of other denominations or the general population. What may have made the scandal more shocking when it first made national headlines in 2002 was not simply the abuse itself, but the way in which it was covered up for many years by Church authorities, including some bishops. In the case of priest John Geoghan, put on trial in Massachusetts in early 2002, documented evidence revealed that Cardinal Bernard Law (1931–), archbishop of Boston, not only overlooked Geoghan's crimes and that of other wayward priests, but shuffled the clergymen from parish to parish without informing those parishes of the priests' sexual offenses. As a result, the abuse of young children in those parishes by Geoghan and others continued for years.

Geoghan was convicted and sentenced to prison. Cardinal Law, under pressure from the public, including many Catholics, resigned in December 2002 and moved to Rome, where he was given an honorific position in the Vatican. While the abuse cases in Boston, the nation's fourth-largest diocese, were the first to come to light, other regions of the country soon had their own cases of abuse by priests. More and more adult victims spoke out about abuse that in many cases had taken place decades before. To date, the Church has paid more than $800 million to victims in reparation. In 2004 alone, the Church paid $139.6 million to victims. Some dioceses have already had to file for bankruptcy.

Church officials have vowed to end the cycle of abuse with strict rules, immediate exposure, and swift expulsion of the offending priests. Nearly every one of the 195 dioceses in the United States have programs in place to educate parishioners about the signs of abuse and to provide aid and support for victims. The Church is trying to put the scandal behind it, but serious damage has been done to its reputation. While pleased that reforms have been instituted, many American Catholics are calling for a greater accountability from other bishops whom they feel protected guilty priests from punishment, at a terrible price. "What we now know is they knew a lot," said Jim Post, president of Voice of the Faithful, a Catholic lay organization, "they did very little and they did a great deal to cover up."

The shrinking parishes

One repercussion of the sex scandal and its enormous cost to the Church is the closing of parishes. Critics claim that the payment of enormous amounts of money to victims has drained the Church coffers of funds needed to maintain parishes. However, this is just one factor in the closings. A shortage of priests to staff the churches is another. So is the flight of many Catholics from the inner city to the suburbs, leaving many urban churches all but empty. Another factor is the serious deterioration of many older churches that the Church cannot afford to repair.

In Boston, Archbishop Sean O'Malley, who replaced Cardinal Law, announced plans in 2004 to close eighty-two parish churches—about a quarter of all those in the diocese. Many faithful parishioners have been saddened and shocked by the closings. Some have participated in prayer vigils and even sit-ins to protest. Some have refused to leave their churches and have occupied buildings twenty-four hours a day to keep them open. While priests have not participated in these demonstrations, some are sympathetic.

A shortage of priests, a shrinking number of parishes, and an international sexual abuse scandal have made the role of the priest in the twenty-first century all the more challenging.

"Our attitude is no, we won't give up," said seventy-five-year-old Doris Giardrillo, who spent a good part of ten days in the sanctuary of Saint Therese in the Boston diocese, praying her rosary. "We're told the archdiocese is hanging tough and won't back down. They're tough, but we're tougher."

The priest shortage

The shortage of priests in the United States has reached a crisis level. There were about 46,000 active priests in the nation in 2005, more than 11,000 fewer than there were in 1975. Nearly a quarter of the 46,000 are older than 70, and the average age is 58. There were 441 priestly ordinations in 2003, compared to 994 in 1965.

Why are fewer men entering the priesthood? Part of the answer lies in ethnic groups, such as the Irish and Italians, whose young men found the priesthood one of the few upwardly mobile careers open to them. Today these ethnic groups have assimilated into American society and have a wealth of other career options open to them. Another reason is the vow of celibacy that many priests, or men considering priesthood, reject. The only priests who may be married at present are those who came to the priesthood after serving as Protestant ministers and who already have wives and children. Some critics, even within the Church, say that celibacy is unnatural and that repressed sexuality is unhealthy and may even have led some priests to child abuse. But others see the vow of celibacy as establishing the marriage of a priest's soul with God, leaving him free of family obligations to better follow in Jesus's footsteps in service to his brothers and sisters.

The shrinking number of priests is not unique to the United States. There is a serious shortage of priests throughout Latin America, Africa, and Asia. Worldwide, more than three thousand parishes are without any priests. The shortage has also affected western Europe, which has one of the highest numbers of Catholics of any continent. Even Ireland, one of the most Catholic countries on earth, has been affected. At one time the Irish exported priests to the United States. Not anymore. Only eight new priests were ordained in Ireland in 2004, and only one seminary now operates there. The shortage reflects a waning of Catholicism's power and authority in that nation. As Ireland has become more prosperous, thanks largely to membership in the European Union (EU)—an economic organization of countries—many citizens have grown less involved with religion and have immersed themselves in the secular world. Mass attendance is down, and the Church no longer has the power and influence it long enjoyed.

An Energized Laity

One of the positive results of these crises is the increasing role the laity has come to play in the Church. Once the Church's "silent majority," the laity reacted to the sexual scandal with righteous anger. Lay groups such as Voice of the Faithful have called for more accountability from Church officials. The growing dialogue between these concerned groups and the Church hierarchy is an encouraging sign for the future. "The bishops and pastors are not used to dealing with this," said Paul F. Lakeland, a religion professor at Jesuit-run Fairfield University in Connecticut. "The laity are [sic] realizing their responsibility as adults."

The laity is not only criticizing, but taking constructive steps to help. To pick up the slack of the priest shortage, lay members are serving as deacons in their parishes, performing many of the roles that priests do, such as bringing Holy Communion to the sick. Others have become associates in religious orders, involved in administration, education, and charitable works. They serve as seculars, without taking the vows of chastity, obedience, and poverty. In a 2002 study, there were about 30,000 lay associates working within the Church, the majority of them female. "The trend has been moving so fast that Rome has not caught up with it and hasn't been issuing rules and regulations," said Sister Patricia Ann Wittberg of the Sisters of Charity in Cincinnati, Ohio. The Church has consistently refused to allow women into the priesthood because Jesus chose only men as his disciples. This rule against women priests was definitely confirmed by Pope John Paul II in the 1980s.

Three schools of Thought

The Catholic Church is not unified in its views, especially in the United States, where many lay Catholics have been independent thinkers for decades. Today there is a great diversity of opinion within the Church, just as there is in the American electorate. If the United States has its blue (liberal Democratic) and red (conservative Republican) states, the Catholic Church in the United States has its own segmented populations.

The conservative wing of the Church receives with religious submission the decisions of the hierarchy. It "thinks with the Church," in the words of Saint Ignatius of Loyola. Conservative Catholics strongly oppose contraception, abortion, homosexuality, and embryonic stem-cell research in which cells from fertilized human eggs are used for research in order to understand and combat cancer and other diseases.

One of the leaders of the conservatives is Father C. John McCloskey III (1954–), a past director of the Catholic Information Center of the Archdiocese of Washington, D.C. A former Wall Street trader, McCloskey became a priest in 1981. In his years in Washington, McCloskey formed strong ties with Republican politicians and sought to make Catholics an influential voting block in national elections. He and a number of conservative bishops warned Catholics not to vote for candidates, such as 2004 Catholic Democratic presidential candidate John Kerry, who support a woman's right to have an abortion.

McCloskey, a member of the Catholic organization Opus Dei, has the reputation of being a maker of converts. He has received into the Church, among others, former abortion-rights champion Doctor Bernard Nathanson; Senator Sam Brownback of Kansas; and Judge Robert H. Bork.

In one of his numerous articles on his Web site, "McCloskey's Perspectives," he contrasts the devout faithful in developing countries, who are often persecuted for their Catholicism, with the Catholics of Europe and the United States, whom he sees as "lightly throwing away centuries of their Christian heritage."

Some of that heritage, according to members of the Church's liberal wing, is excess baggage that deserves to be thrown away for the betterment of the Church and the world. Few members of the liberal wing are more outspoken than James Carroll (1943–), a former priest who became an award-winning and best-selling novelist and writer about the Church and its problems.

In his book *Toward a New Catholic Church: The Promise of Reform* (2002), Carroll proposes a Vatican III Council to pursue sweeping reforms that would reduce the authority of the Vatican and empower the laity, remove politics from the Church's agenda, and have the Church publicly acknowledge its "sins" of sexism and anti-Semitism, among others. Most controversial of Carroll's proposals is the redefining of Jesus Christ, emphasizing his role as a teacher of God's will rather than a savior.

A committed activist, Carroll has compared the imperial Rome of Jesus's era to the imperial power of the United States today. "A story of Jesus born into a land oppressed by a hated military occupation might prompt an examination of the American occupation of Iraq," he wrote in one of his weekly columns in the *Boston Globe* at Christmastime in 2004.

The traditionalists form a third major group of contemporary Catholics. They reject the Vatican II and often refuse to submit to papal and episcopal authority. Promoting the old Latin Mass is their top priority.

The late, excommunicated Archbishop Marcel Lefebvre was the most prominent traditionalist leader. The filmmaker and actor Mel Gibson, who recently produced and directed *The Passion of the Christ*, is a prominent Catholic who seems to be aligned with traditionalism.

It is estimated that there are about a million schismatic traditionalists worldwide today, who have their own separate Church. They may be relatively few and scattered, but they should not be dismissed as unimportant.

The global church

If there is one issue that these three divergent groups might agree on, with varying degrees of enthusiasm, it is that geographically the Church of the twenty-first century is a far cry from the Church that existed for the last twenty centuries.

"We are currently living through one of the transforming moments in the history of religion worldwide," wrote Philip Jenkins in his book *The Next Christendom: The Coming of Global Christianity* (2002). "Over the past century, however, the center of gravity in the Christian world has shifted inexorably southward, to Africa, Asia and Latin America." Statistics bear out his claim. The largest number of Catholics today reside in Latin America, where Brazil and Mexico alone account for nearly a quarter of the world's 1.1 billion Catholics. But the greatest growth in the Church is in Africa and Asia. In the Congo, for example, there has been a 20 percent growth of Catholics

This Ethiopian boy is reading his Bible in a mountain monastery. The African continent, along with Asia, has seen the greatest growth in the number of new Catholics in recent decades.

in the population from 1970 to 2005. In the same time period in Micronesia, a group of many islands in the western Pacific, there has been a growth rate of 37 percent.

Pope John Paul's many visits to countries in the developing world have drawn attention to these places, where Catholic evangelism is booming. In his apostolic letter of 2001, *Novo Millennio Ineunte,* meaning "At the Beginning of the New Millennium," the late pope called for a "New Evangelization" throughout the world. But Catholics are not the only Christian missionaries in developing nations. Protestant evangelicals have converted many people in South and Central America who were formerly Catholic over the past thirty years. Young and energetic, with a personal message of salvation for the world's people, these Protestants are a threat to the Catholics who for too long took their Latin American brethren for granted.

One piece of supporting evidence is the few Latin Americans, Africans, and Asians who are represented in the College of Cardinals in Rome. Among these cardinals from developing nations is Cardinal Francis Arinze (1933–) of Nigeria, who served admirably as the head of the Pontifical Council for Interreligious Dialogue for eighteen years. A humble man who is seen as a peacemaker in the Church, Cardinal Arinze was first appointed the head of the Congregation for Divine Worship and the Discipline of Sacraments by Pope John Paul II in 2002. As the head of this permanent committee, he oversees the regulation and promotion of the sacred liturgy. Pope Benedict then named him one of the top six cardinals, called cardinal-bishops, in 2005. It is men like Arinze who may bring a fresh perspective and a renewed sense of mission to the Church.

In the steps of christ

There are no easy solutions to the problems of the Roman Catholic Church. But the Church has survived hard times before—times of corruption, persecution, and apathy. For the faithful, the Catholic Church remains Christ's kingdom on earth. In their eyes it will not only survive, but overcome. Brian Bashista, a young American priest, sums up this optimistic message. "We already know the end of the story," he said. "God will triumph. The Church will triumph. That doesn't mean that the present trials aren't there. . . . But the threats will never succeed. The essentials will never change. How do we know that? Because Christ said so."

Catholics raise a white cross on a mountain peak near Tucson, Arizona, at sunrise on Good Friday in memory of Jesus's crucifixion.

TIME LINE

6 B.C.E.

Jesus is born in Bethlehem in Palestine.

C.E. 30

Jesus starts his public ministry and gathers a group of disciples.

about 33

Jesus is crucified in Jerusalem by the Romans and is resurrected from the dead.

40s–50s

Paul makes his three missionary journeys to Asia Minor, Macedonia, and Greece to spread the Christian message and found new Christian churches.

64–67

Peter and Paul are martyred in Rome during Nero's persecution of Christians.

100

John, the last surviving apostle, dies.

303

The last of the major ancient persecutions of Christians is begun by Emperor Diocletian.

313

Roman emperor Constantine the Great issues the Edict of Milan, granting Christians the right to practice their faith.

325

The first ecumenical council meets at Nicea and affirms the divine nature of Jesus Christ.

330

Constantine moves the capital of Christianity from Rome to Constantinople, now called Istanbul in present-day Turkey.

392

The emperor Theodosius establishes Christianity as Rome's state religion.

426

Augustine completes his book *The City of God*.

431

The Ecumenical Council of Ephesus declares Mary the "Godbearer" or mother of God.

476

Rome is conquered by Germanic invaders.

529

Benedict founds the monastic Benedictine Order at Monte Cassino.

596

Benedictine missionary monks are sent by Pope Gregory I to convert the English.

732

Charles Martel stops the Muslim advance at Poitiers, France, saving Christian Europe.

800

Pope Leo III crowns French king Charlemagne emperor of the Romans and defender of Christianity.

962

The Holy Roman empire is established in western Europe.

1054

The Western Roman Church and the Eastern Byzantine Church split.

1095

The participants in the first Crusade leave Europe to recapture the Holy Land from the Turks.

about 1100

The University of Bologna, the first modern Western university, is founded in Italy.

1231

The Inquisition is established by Pope Gregory IX.

1274

Thomas Aquinas completes his monumental work *Summa Theologiae*.

1309

The papacy moves from Rome to Avignon, France, and remains there for sixty-eight years.

1378–1415

The Great Western Schism divides the Church. Three individuals claim papal authority in Rome, Avignon, and Pisa.

1414–1418

The Ecumenical Council of Constance reinstates Rome as home of the true pope, but fails in its attempt to declare itself his superior.

1508

Renaissance artist Michelangelo begins work on frescoes for the Vatican's Sistine Chapel.

1517

Martin Luther, a German monk, posts Ninety-five Theses on the Wittenberg Church door, beginning the Protestant Reformation.

1534

Ignatius Loyola founds the Society of Jesus, whose members are known as Jesuits.

1545–1563

The Council of Trent marks the start of the Counter-Reformation.

1570

Pope Pius V excommunicates Queen Elizabeth I of England, the last time to date that a pope excommunicates a head of state.

1572

Thousands of French Huguenots (Protestants) are killed by Catholics in Paris on August 24 in the Saint Bartholomew's Day Massacre and for weeks afterward throughout France.

1618

The Thirty Years War begins in Europe between Protestants and Catholics.

1632

The colony of Maryland is established as a haven for persecuted English Catholics.

1773

Pope Clement XIV bans the Jesuits.

1787–1799

Strong anti-religious feelings during the French Revolution lead to the death and exile of many priests and the confiscation of Church property.

1789

John Carroll is elected the first Catholic bishop in the United States.

1791

The U.S. Constitution's First Amendment grants religious freedom, using a phrase from the charter of Catholic Maryland, "the free exercise thereof."

1809

Elizabeth Ann Seton founds the Sisters of Charity in Maryland; Napoléon takes Pope Pius VII prisoner.

1814

Jesuits are restored in the Catholic Church.

1846

Pope Pius IX begins his long reign of reactionary conservatism in the face of the attacks of revolutionaries and their armies.

1869–1870

The First Vatican Council defines papal infallibility.

1878

Pope Leo XIII comes to power. His encyclical *Rerum Novarum* approves of labor unions, condemns child labor and harsh working conditions, and attempts to modernize the Church.

1928

Al Smith becomes the first Catholic to run as a major political party candidate for the U.S. presidency.

1939–1945

The Church under Pope Pius XII maintains neutrality in World War II, but also saves about 800,000 Jews from being murdered by the Nazis.

1946–1991

Ruling Communist governments in Eastern Europe suppress and persecute the Catholic Church.

1958

Pope John XXIII is elected.

1960

Democrat John F. Kennedy becomes the first Catholic to be elected U.S. president.

1962–1965

Vatican Council II, summoned by Pope John, creates sweeping reforms in the Church.

1968

Pope Paul VI issues *Humanae Vitae*, an encyclical that reaffirms traditional Church teaching against artificial means of birth control.

1978

John Paul II, a Pole, becomes the first pope from Eastern Europe.

1981

John Paul II is shot by a Turkish terrorist in an assassination attempt.

1988

Retired archbishop and Church traditionalist Marcel Lefebvre of France is excommunicated for ordaining four men as bishops.

1991

The Soviet Union dissolves itself on December 8. In the next decade, the Catholic Church experiences a revival throughout eastern Europe.

1992

The first universal catechism for adults in 450 years is published, *The Catechism of the Catholic Church.*

2001

John Paul II calls for a "New Evangelization" among Catholics in his apostolic letter *Novo Millennio Ineunte*.

2002

The scandal involving priests abusing children breaks in the United States in January. In December, Cardinal Bernard Law of Boston resigns as archbishop of Boston over his role in the scandal.

2005

On April 2, Pope John Paul II dies at age eighty-four. Cardinal Joseph Ratzinger is elected Pope Benedict XVI on April 19.

GLOSSARY

Advent—The four weeks before Christmas. For Christians, a special time of preparation for Christ's birth.

annulment—Declaring a Catholic marriage invalid for one or more reasons.

anointing of the sick—The rite of administering holy oil to a seriously sick person to grant forgiveness, healing, and comfort; one of the seven sacraments.

apostolic succession—A tenet of Catholic faith that justifies the Church's authority by the long, unbroken line of bishops going back to the apostles.

autocephalous—The independent status of each Eastern Orthodox church, which is led by its own patriarch.

baptism—A rite that cleanses a person of original sin and confers sanctifying grace; one of the seven sacraments.

beatified—For holy persons to be declared "Blessed" by the Church.

bishop—A senior clergyman, usually in charge of a diocese.

bull—A papal decree.

canonize—Officially declare someone a saint of the Church.

cathedral—A church in which a bishop usually celebrates the sacraments.

celebrant—A priest or bishop who performs the Mass or other church rite.

cenobite—A religious male or female who lives a communal life with other monks or nuns.

chrism—A holy oil used in the sacrament of confirmation.

cloister—A secluded monastery or inner part of a monastery.

College of Cardinals—The body of high churchmen, almost always bishops, who advise the pope and elect a new pope when one dies.

confirmation—A ceremony that confirms a permanent grace of the soul and completes baptism; one of the seven sacraments.

crèche—An arrangement of figures to represent the birth of Jesus.

Curia—An administrative body in the Vatican that assists the pope in running the Church.

deacon—A level of ordained clergy below priest that can perform certain functions within the Church such as presiding over and witnessing marriages.

Deuterocanonical—A group of Greek Old Testament writings in the Catholic Bible that are not included in the Hebrew or most Protestant bibles; Protestants call these books Apocrypha.

diocese—The basic administrative unit or district of the Church under the care of a bishop.

doxology—A liturgical formula of praise to God.

Eastern Orthodox Church—The branch of the Christian Church that broke away from the Roman Church in 1054 and has its own customs, rites, and traditions.

ecumenical council—A general meeting of all bishops that is called or approved by the pope.

ecumenicalism—A movement to promote Christian unity throughout the world.

encyclical—A papal letter sent to all bishops of the Church.

eremite—A religious male or female who lives in a closed community and spends most of his or her time in solitary prayer, work, study, and contemplation.

Eucharist—The sacrament that commemorates Jesus's Last Supper; it can also refer to the eucharistic elements—bread and wine.

ex cathedra—From the seat of authority, referring to the pope's pronouncements on matters of faith that are said to be always right.

excommunication—The act of cutting off a Catholic from communion with the Church.

filioque—The belief in Christian theology that the Holy Spirit proceeds from both God, the father, and Jesus Christ, the son.

Gospels—The four books of the Bible's New Testament that tell of the life of Jesus Christ.

grace—The freely given, unmerited love of God; the influence of God operating in humans to strengthen them; a prayer said before meals.

heresy—A belief or practice contrary to Church doctrine.

holy days of obligation—Specially designated days on which Catholics are required to attend Mass.

holy orders—The initiation of men into the ministry as deacons, priests, or bishops; one of the seven sacraments.

Holy Trinity—The Catholic doctrine that holds God to be three beings (the Father, Son, and Holy Spirit) with one divine nature.

holy water—Water that has been blessed by a priest.

homily—A brief sermon or talk that is part of the Mass or other religious rite or ceremony.

host—The individual piece of consecrated unleavened bread used in Holy Communion.

icon—A religious painting in the Eastern Orthodox Church.

iconostasis—A partition that separates the sanctuary and the congregation in an Eastern Orthodox Church.

laicize—To strip a priest who has proved unworthy of his office of his right to function as a priest.

laity—All members of the Church who are not clergy.

Lent—The forty days, not counting Sundays, before Easter; a special time of reflection and penance.

liturgy—A form of public religious worship; a series of religious rites.

Mass—A religious rite that makes present and celebrates the death and resurrection of Jesus.

matrimony—The spiritual union of man and woman before God for mutual support and procreation; one of the seven sacraments.

monastery—An often secluded religious community whose members have taken holy vows.

monk—A male monastic.

mystery—A significant event in the life of Jesus or the Virgin Mary.

New Testament—The second part of the Bible which depicts events from the birth of Jesus Christ to about 100 C.E.

nun—A female monastic.

Old Testament—The first part of the Bible that depicts events from God's creation of the world to the first century B.C.E.

parish—A Catholic community centered around a church and run by a pastor.

parishioners—All the Catholics who live in a parish.

pastor—A priest who is in charge of a parish and serves as its spiritual leader.

patriarch—The supreme religious leader in an Eastern Orthodox or Eastern Catholic Church; formerly, the archbishop of a few ancient centers of the Roman Catholic Church.

patriarchate—The spiritual community over which a patriarch rules.

penance—A public confession of sins and forgiveness dictated by God's representative, the priest; one of the seven sacraments.

pontiff—The pope.

pope—The visible head and highest authority in the Roman Catholic Church.

presbyters—Priests.

priest—A member of the Catholic clergy who can celebrate the Mass and minister or give other sacraments.

purgatory—A temporary place of suffering in the afterlife, where those with some debt of sin are cleansed before entering heaven.

relic—A part of the body of Jesus Christ or a saint of the Church, or one of their possessions.

religious—A person or several people bound by monastic vows.

rosary beads—A string of beads used for prayer and meditation.

sacrament—An outward sign in words and gestures that communicates inward grace.

sacramental—A rite of the Church that honors and elevates material objects and activities to a higher spiritual level.

saint—A deceased holy person recognized by the Church as being in heaven and worthy of imitation.

sanctuary—The part of a church that surrounds the altar.

scholastics—Systematic philosophers and theologians, particularly those of medieval times; contemporary ones are often called neoscholastics.

scrutinies—Special ballots used by cardinals when voting for a new pope.

sees—Religious seats or centers.

seminary—A college where men are trained to become priests.

synod—A local meeting or council attended by clergy and sometimes laity.

tabernacle—An ornamental receptacle on the altar that holds the Eucharist.

transubstantiation—The mystery of transforming bread and wine into the body and blood of Jesus Christ during Mass.

Vatican City—The small independent territory within the city of Rome that is the pope's residence and the Church's headquarters.

votive candles—Candles in a church sanctuary lit by a loved one for a friend or family member.

FURTHER RESOURCES

BOOKS

Benedict XVI. *Milestones: Memoirs 1927–1977.* San Francisco: Ignatius Press, 1998.

Carroll, James. *Toward a New Catholic Church: The Promise of Reform.* Boston: Houghton Mifflin, 2002.

The Cathechism of the Catholic Church, 2nd ed. Washington, D.C.: United States Conference of Catholic Bishops, 1997.

Delaney, John J., ed. *Saints for All Seasons: Personal Portraits of Favorite Saints by 20 Outstanding Catholic Authors.* Garden City, NY: Doubleday, 1978.

Fisher, James T. *Catholics in America.* New York: Oxford University Press, 2000.

Grady, Thomas, and Paula Huston, eds. *Signatures of Grace: Catholic Writers on the Sacraments.* New York: Penguin, 2001.

Groeschel, Father Benedict J. *There Are No Accidents: In All Things Trust in God.* Huntington, IN: Our Sunday Visitor Publishing Division, 2004.

Ignatius Bible. Revised, standard version, Catholic edition. San Francisco: Ignatius Press, 1994.

John Paul II, Pope. *Memory and Identity: Conversations at the Dawn of a Millennium.* New York: Rizzoli, 2005.

Kenny, John J. *Now That You Are a Catholic: An Informal Guide to Catholic Customs, Traditions, and Practices.* Mahwah, NJ: Paulist Press, 2003.

Kung, Hans. *The Catholic Church: A Short History.* New York: Modern Library, 2003.

Le Goulard, Veronica Namoy. *A Memory for Wonders: A True Story.* San Francisco: Ignatius Press, 1993.

O'Gorman, Bob, and Mary Faulkner. *The Complete Idiot's Guide to Understanding Catholicism.* New York: Macmillan USA, 2003.

Parker, Victoria. *The Vatican: And Other Christian Holy Places.* Chicago: Raintree, 2003.

Weigel, George. *Letters to a Young Catholic.* New York: Basic Books, 2004.

FILMS (DVDs)

From Jesus to Christ—The First Christians. Paramount Home Video, 2005.

The Passion of the Christ. Fox Home Entertainment, 2004.

Pope John Paul II: 1920–2005. BBC Warner, 2005.

Wonders of the Vatican Library. Melee, 2004.

WEB SITES

Catholic Information Center on Internet Home Page

http://www.catholic.net/

This site contains a wealth of information including global Catholic news from Rome, U.S. Catholic news, and a pope page.

The Holy See

http://www.vatican.va/

The official Vatican Web site is beautifully designed and contains biographies of important popes, their encyclicals and other writings, the catalogs of the Vatican Library, lives of the saints of the Church, and much more. In English as well as Italian and other languages.

Society of Jesus USA

http://www.jesuit.org/

The official site of the American branch of one of the largest and most influential religious orders in the Catholic Church.

United States Conference of Catholic Bishops

http://www.nccbuscc.org/

The official site of the Conference of Catholic Bishops includes the latest Catholic news, daily readings from the Bible, events in the Church, and much more.

SOURCE NOTES

CHAPTER ONE:

p. 13: "Why do you look. . . ." *Life Application Study Bible* (NIV translation), (Wheaton, IL: Tyndale House, 1991), pp. 1861–1862.

p. 14: "Blessed are the poor in spirit. . . ." *Study Bible,* pp. 1651–1652.

p. 14: "You have heard. . . ." *Study Bible,* p. 1656.

p. 14: "Why do you look. . . ." *Study Bible,* p. 1660.

p. 14: "Ask and it will be given . . ." *Study Bible,* p. 1660.

p. 19: "Peter has spoken through Leo!" Hubert Jedin, *Ecumenical Councils of the Catholic Church: An Historical Survey,* (New York: Herder and Herder, 1960), p. 37.

p. 22: "for every letter, line, . . ." Anne Fremantle, *Age of Faith* (New York: Time-Life Books, 1965) p. 48.

p. 29: "Unless I am convicted by Scripture. . . ." Edith Simon, *The Reformation* (New York: Time-Life Books, 1966), p. 43.

p. 31: "Even if my own father. . . . " Simon, p. 109.

p. 35: ". . . the first end I propose. . . ." *Liturgy of the Hours I* (Totowa, NJ: Catholic Book Publishing, 2000), p. 1690.

p. 36: "I recognize no power. . . ." James T. Fisher, *Catholics in America* (New York: Oxford University Press, 2000), p. 106.

CHAPTER TWO:

p. 44: "Turn from evil. . . ." *Study Bible,* p. 938.

p. 45: "Rejoice in the Lord always. . . ." *Study Bible,* p. 2153.

p. 53: "To judge the living. . . ." *Study Bible,* p. 2263.

p. 53: "Behold, I am coming soon!" *Study Bible,* p. 2334.

p. 53: "with the Lord a day is . . ." *Study Bible,* p. 2271.

CHAPTER FOUR:

p. 61: "Do this in remembrance of me." *Study Bible,* p. 1854.

p. 61: "the source and summit . . ." *The Catechism of the Catholic Church*, 2nd ed. (Washington, D.C.: United States Conference of Catholic Bishops, 1997), no. 1324.

p. 63: "Our gifts of bread and wine . . ." Ron Hansen, *Signatures of Grace: Catholic Writers on the Sacraments*, (New York: Penguin, 2001), p. 88.

p. 68: "At the center of each. . . ." Mary Gordon, *Signatures of Grace* pp. 207–208.

p. 73: "no one else." John C. Iannone, *The Mystery of the Shroud of Turin: New Scientific Evidence* (Staten Island, NY: Alba House, 1998), p. xi.

CHAPTER SIX:

p. 85: "God's Rottweiler. . . ." George Weigel, "The Real Benedict," *Newsweek*, May 2, 2005, p. 48.

p. 85: "He has a very. . . ." Christopher Dickey and Melinda Henneberger "The Vision of Benedict XVI," *Newsweek,* May 2, 2005, p. 49.

p. 87: "What we now know. . . ." Elizabeth Mehren, "162 Boston Priests Accused in Sex Scandal," *Los Angeles Times*, February 27, 2004, A28.

p. 89: "Our attitude is no. . . ." Katie Zezima, "Parish Closings Inspire Prayer Vigils and Sit-Ins," *The New York Times,* November 6, 2004, p. A11.

p. 90: "The bishops and pastors are not used. . . ." Patrick Healy, "Fissures in a Grand Church," *The New York Times,* August 29, 2004, p. 33.

p. 91: "The trend has been moving. . . ." Marek Fuchs, "Lay Members Help Ease a Crisis in Catholic Orders," *The New York Times*, January 8, 2005, p. B5.

p. 92: "A story of Jesus. . . ." James Carroll, "The Politics of the Christmas story." *Boston Globe*, December 21, 2004.

p. 93: "We are currently living. . . Latin America." Philip Jenkins, quoted by McCloskey, "Christianity Tomorrow."

p. 96: "We already know the end. . . ." Jennifer Egan, "Why a Priest," The *New York Times Sunday Magazine,* April 4, 1999, p. 59.

INDEX

Page numbers in **boldface** are illustrations.

sacramentals, 68

sacraments, 61–68, 80

Sacred College, 54

saints, 27–29, 49

  American, 35

  patron saints, 51

  relics of, 70–71

  See also specific saints

salvation, 52

Saul of Tarsus. *See* Paul

schism

  within Europe, 26–27

  Roman and Orthodox, 17, 22–23, 82

scholasticism, 23–24

schools, 68

secularism, 32

Sermon on the Mount, 14

Serra, Junipero, 34

Seton, Elizabeth Ann (Saint), 35

sexual abuse, 10, 86–87, 89

shrines, 71

Shroud of Turin, 71, **72**, 73

sin, 49, 63, 64, 65

Sistine Chapel, 23, 55

Smith, Al, 37

social policies, 10, 33, 42

Spain, 21, 31

stem-cell research, 10, 91

Swiss Guard, 55

Synod of Bishops, 56

Ten Commandments, 44–47, **46**

tertiaries, 60

Theodosius I, 17

theological virtues, 47

theology. *See* beliefs

Thirty Years War, 32

Thomas Aquinas (Saint), 23–24, **24**

Three Wise Men, 74

traditionalists, 93

transubstantiation, **62**, 63

trends, 10, 87–96

Turks, 22, 25

Ukraine, 83

United States, 10, 34–37, 71–74, 78, 86–89, 91–93, **97**

Urban II (pope), 22, 25

Urban VI (pope), 26–27

Vatican City, 54–55, 57

Vatican I, 33

Vatican II, 31, 38–39, 40, 48, 65, 67

vigils, 69, 75, 87–89

Virgin Mary (mother of Jesus), 12, 27–29, 49, **50**, 71

virtue, 44–47

Voice of the Faithful, 90

Voltaire, François, 32

Vulgate, 19

war, 10, 42

women, 80, **81**, 90–91

  See also Mary Magdalene; nuns; Seton, Elizabeth Ann; Virgin Mary

workers, 33, 51

World Council of Churches, 83

World War II, 37

Wyszynski, Stefan (cardinal), 38

ABOUT THE AUTHOR

STEVEN OTFINOSKI has written more than 120 books for young readers. His many biographies include books about Jesse Jackson, Oprah Winfrey, John Wilkes Booth, Nelson Mandela, and Boris Yeltsin. He has also written books on geography, world history, rock music, public speaking, and writing.

He is the author of *Marco Polo: To China and Back, Francisco Coronado: In Search of the Seven Cities of Gold, Vasco Nuñez de Balboa: Discoverer of the Pacific, Juan Ponce de León: Discoverer of Florida,* and *Henry Hudson: In Search of the Northwest Passage* in the Great Explorations series. His other works for Marshall Cavendish include the twelve-volume transportation series for early readers Here We Go! and books on New Hampshire, Georgia, Maryland, and Washington State in the Celebrate the States and It's My State! series.

Two of his books, *Triumph and Terror: The French Revolution* and *Poland: Nation in Transition*, were chosen as Books for the Teen Age by the New York Public Library.

Otfinoski is also a produced playwright and has his own theater company History Alive! which brings plays about American history to schoolchildren. He lives with his wife, Beverly, and their two children in Connecticut.